DEATH DISASTERS & DOCTORS' DILEMMAS

Lest I Forget

Published by Dr John Anthony Cotterill

Copyright © Dr John Anthony Cotterill 2022

Dr John Anthony Cotterill has asserted his right under the Copyright, Designs and Patents Act, 1988, to be identified as the author of this work.

Paperback ISBN: 978-1-7391233-2-1
eBook ISBN: 978-1-7391233-1-4

Cover design and typeset by SpiffingCovers

DEATH
DISASTERS
& DOCTORS'
DILEMMAS
Lest I Forget

DR JOHN ANTHONY COTTERILL

Contents

ACKNOWLEDGEMENTS

Thanks must go to a long-suffering wife and apologies to my children for spending too little time at home with them. My eldest daughter Suzannah, was an invaluable help to me in producing much of the manuscript, correcting some of my bad English on the way. Dawn Lippa tolerated my many attempts at writing this book and typed the original and final manuscript. Thanks must go to my many patients, teachers and colleagues who taught me that there is much more about dermatology than skin.

FORWARD

Dr Cotterill was a Consultant Dermatologist at the General Infirmary in Leeds (LGI) from 1973 – 1995 having a particular interest in the emotional, psychological and psychiatric aspects of skin disease and also the interrelationship of light on the skin. He established a laser unit at the LGI, one of the first in the UK principally to treat children and adults with port wine stains.

Dr Cotterill became increasingly frustrated by poor NHS management and resigned from the NHS in 1995.

INTRODUCTION

I first put pen to paper to record some of the more memorable events in my life for my three daughters and two grandchildren. I showed the rough manuscript to some of my friends and dermatological colleagues who all urged me to try and publish it. I am grateful to them all for the encouragement and valued criticisms they made.

I enjoyed my life as a medical student, junior doctor and finally consultant dermatologist enormously and if I had the chance, I would do the same all over again. Back in the 60's, 70's, 80's and 90's the clinics were enormous and the work as a result very tiring. Clinics of 50 patients or more were common place and my record clinic was seeing 148 patients during one afternoon when my colleagues all left the department for a meeting in Sheffield leaving me to do my own and their two clinics.

Despite the patient numbers morale was high and there was little talk of 'burnout' and life in hospital for junior doctors in training centred around the mess and the surgical and medical 'firm' system so you belonged to a family and had a home and felt valued, the only downside was very long hours. There was always a colleague to talk to especially in the mess dining room and a mess dinner every month to let your hair down. Hospitals were not alcohol-free zones as now and the consultant would be invited to carve the turkey at Christmas in the wards under his or her care and take a drink with sister and staff.

How different are things now. No in house dining room, no firm, little opportunity to talk to colleagues because of a shift system often at unsociable hours. Sadly, there continues in most hospitals, to be nowhere to sleep at night except in your car which the hospital will charge you for parking. Blankets may be available on a cold night, but it is not unusual for the hospital to charge you for these. Kitchens are often closed for instance during Christmas and it is the norm especially for juniors to work much longer than the allocated shift hours and doctors are known to be accident prone whilst returning home after long nights at work. The possibility of providing transport home after a long and exacting night shift has not been explored by most hospital trusts. Married couples may be allocated training posts many miles away from each other and with different shifts leaving little chance to cement a marriage. It is said that nearly 20% of juniors elect not to continue to practise.

The over-managed and over-politicised NHS is a current disaster. The NHS has never really recovered from the massive and disastrous management changes imposed on the then well performing NHS in the early 1970's by Sir Keith Joseph referred to as the 'Mad Monk' by Private Eye. These management changes were compounded by the Salmon report introducing serious but deleterious management changes to nursing care. The net result, years later, and after many more disastrous management changes is a serious shortage of nurses, doctors and midwives. Nurses pay is poor and fails to keep up with inflation.

It is against this background that the stories that follow have occurred. Names have been changed where necessary and I hope the reader will get as much enjoyment out of the book as I have had writing it.

December 2021

CHILDHOOD

I was born in 1940. My mother told me that this was in Jessops Maternity Hospital in Sheffield which no longer exists, but my birth certificate records I was born at home. At this time the country was at war. Sheffield was being bombed on a regular basis to try and destroy the steel industry. My early months, therefore, were spent during anxious nights in an air raid shelter at the bottom of the garden. Talking to my mother later I think she was very frightened on her own in the air raid shelter lit only by a candle. My father meanwhile, had joined the home guard and he was armed with a wooden rifle. During war games in Sheffield on one occasion my father 'refused to die' when a member of another home guard unit, also armed with a wooden rifle, proclaimed my father dead. During the war my father got to throw one live hand grenade and was eventually issued with a rifle and live ammunition. After the war my father's army greatcoat was used to keep me warm in bed during the winter months as we had no central heating in the house.

School at the age of four was a bit traumatic. I can remember that on the first day I was caned over the knuckles because I was unable to open a tin of crayons. The crayons were in an old tobacco tin which I failed to prise open. I had all the usual illnesses including measles which left me deaf in the left ear. Doctors cost money in those days so I was medicated by my mother. I was sent to school in a liberty bodice as were many of the boys of my age, but this did nothing for the masculine side of my personality. I also had to wear a piece of camphor around my neck, which was believed by my mother to prevent coughs and colds and the aroma from it certainly kept peers at bay. I was regularly given yellow eye ointment which contains mercury. This is not a good element to be exposed to. Any temperature or sore throat was treated with Beecham's Powders which contained aspirin. It is now known that aspirin should not be given to children under twelve years of age because of the risk of serious or even fatal liver disease. On a happier note, any hint of a cold would be treated by a little whisky with honey and warm water before going to bed. Fenning's Fever cure was another favourite of my mother. In reality this was dilute nitric acid, and I can still feel my teeth tingle as the acid attacked the enamel. Friar's Balsam was used for a chest infection. A few drops of this balsam was dripped into a bowl of hot water, a towel was placed over your head and you had to inhale the medicated stream for five or ten minutes. Kaolin poultices were also popular especially if it was thought you had pleurisy. Tonics were administered on a regular basis and some of these in the nineteen forties almost certainly contained arsenic.

Before I went to school on my way out of the house, I was 'dish-clothed' on my face and neck by my mother. The dish cloth smelt horrible, often of cabbage, and I still have a phobia about dish cloths which are known to be great purveyors of bacteria. In addition, just before I was going through the door my mother would grab my hair, pulling my head back to make my mouth more accessible and I was given a large spoonful of cod liver oil. I can remember my father took Andrew's Liver Salts each morning on a regular basis for 'inner cleanliness'.

In Sheffield, there was a belief that tar fumes were good for you and especially if you had chest problems. I can still remember being held over a steaming bubbling vat of molten tar for my health's sake. The aroma from tar is now known to be full of carcinogens but it is possible that this early exposure to the aroma of tar may have influenced my choice of becoming a dermatologist. Happily, skin departments no longer smell of tar.

Each weekend my father would take me to visit his stepsister and her husband, Horace. Horace was a park keeper and lived in a house in Norfolk Park in Sheffield. There was no bath in the house and the toilet was outside. When we arrived Horace, totally naked would get into a large zinc tub which had been prepared by his wife Gladys with hot water and he would sit in this zinc tub in front of the fire for half an hour or so washing himself including his 'best bits' and from time to time Gladys would bring some more hot water to make the procedure reasonably comfortable.

Horace would then get out of the bath towel himself down, dress and then began squeezing large senile comedones from his face in front of the mirror. It is possible again that this early experience of dermatological problems may have influenced my choice of becoming a dermatologist. I have to admit I do enjoy squeezing things.

Horace was an expert at playing the spoons and also playing bones. He used to perform at various Working Men's Clubs around the city and when he died, he left his bones to me. I regret to say I have not become particularly proficient, but I think the bones were derived from a sheep.

A GOOD DERMATOLOGIST?

Jack:

Jack was a 67-year-old retired railway man living in Harrogate. He developed psoriasis some years before retiring. Psoriasis is a common skin condition affecting up to 5% of the UK population and is characterised by red, scaly and often itchy skin varying a great deal in severity. In some individuals there is minimal involvement, for example the knees and elbows, whilst in a significant minority the condition is severe affecting large body areas. This was the clinical situation with Jack whose psoriasis became much worse after he retired as a railway man.

Jack loved his job and the company of his workmates and he greatly missed this part of his life after he retired. I thought this could explain the worsening of his psoriasis, so I encouraged Jack to go to the shunting yard when he felt like it, to try to resume, to some extent, his previous social life at work.

Despite taking my advice, the psoriasis remained a big problem, necessitating daily treatment in the outpatient psoriasis bathrooms and because his psoriasis was extensive, the treatment given by the nurses would take two or three hours every day five days per week.

The bathroom treatment consisted of a tar bath followed by controlled exposure to ultraviolet light and finally the application of a paste containing dithranol to the involved areas. This paste had to be applied with obsessive care just to the affected areas because it would both burn and stain normal skin. Finally, talc was applied to the whole body which was then dressed with stockinette. This was a slow and laborious process, and the bathroom nurses were specially trained to carry it out.

Normally the psoriasis would clear on average in about three weeks, leaving a brown skin in the involved areas which would persist for several weeks more.

Jack's psoriasis, however, continued to relapse and I only learnt later that his wife had died, another possible factor in pathogenesis.

After battling with Jack's psoriasis for two years, on a daily basis, the bathroom nurses came to see me and begged me to try a different treatment approach. Jack was spending large parts of the day in the bathrooms, and even after his treatment had finished, just talking to the nurses and making it difficult for them to get on with other patients.

I agreed with the nurses that we had to try something else, so I put Jack on an oral treatment with a drug called hydroxyurea, which was often effective in patients with extensive difficult psoriasis. However, this drug could depress the bone marrow so regular blood counts were necessary especially initially. I arranged regular blood counts every two weeks for Jack and gave him an appointment to see me again in six weeks.

When he came to my clinic I was delighted. For the first time in years, Jack's skin was completely clear of psoriasis. I felt I had been a really good dermatologist. The bathroom nurses were also delighted and asked, "why hadn't I done this earlier"?

I arranged to see Jack in another six weeks, but he failed to attend the clinic. For Jack this was very unusual. Tragically I found out later, a day or two before Jack was due to see me, he had gone down to the shunting yards and jumped in front of one of the engines, killing himself instantly.

Postscript:

Why did Jack do this? What was the reason for this awful tragedy?

On reflection, by being 'a good dermatologist' I had removed Jack from the social contact of the bathroom nurses, which he had enjoyed weekly since his wife's death, and this contact had become so important for him. I concluded that in being a good mechanistic dermatologist, I had also been a rather poor doctor, I had failed Jack.

The commonest reaction to psoriasis is reactive depression, which usually remits when the psoriasis goes. Even the smallest psoriatic lesion on an important body image area such as the glans penis in a male or the genital area or face in a female can lead to the most profound anxiety and reactive depression.

However, for Jack, his psoriasis had, in a way become an emotional crutch which I had removed. The art of medicine is not easy.

Eliza

About thirty years ago I was asked to do a domiciliary visit on a patient by Dr Mary Wells. Dr Mary, as all the patients referred to her, was a much loved General Practitioner of the old school and I first met her when I came to Leeds as a tutor in dermatology, a university appointment.

I bought a nice semi-detached house with a big garden in Adel in North Leeds for £4,250.00, but my salary at that time was just over £1,000.00 per year. Over the years bank managers had always accepted that young doctors would require a hefty overdraft, and this was the case with me. All was well until a Tory chancellor, Selwyn Lloyd, decided to tighten the UK economy and one of his budget proposals was that overdrafts had to be paid off. To try and pay off my mortgage I did some medical market research and also a locum three times per week for Dr Mary. In addition, my wife worked as a part time sister at night in a Leeds Chest Hospital. Despite all this extra income, we remained desperately poor, and I recall we had no stair carpet and three young children.

I got to know Dr Mary well whilst working as a locum and she tried very hard to entice me into her practice as a partner. Anyway, that was not to be and in 1973 I was appointed a Consultant Dermatologist at Leeds General Infirmary.

The patient I was asked to see by Dr Mary, Eliza, lived in Church Fenton, a very old East Yorkshire village not far from Selby. When I arrived at her house, an Elizabethan cottage, there was an incredible white mantle around the house due to thousands of snowdrops. Even though it was spring it looked as though it had just snowed.

I went into the old house and climbed a ladder to Eliza's bedroom. I was accompanied by Dr Mary who told me Eliza was 95 years old and had worked as a district nurse. She was one of the first nurses in England to gain State Registered status (SRN) and I recall the number on her nursing badge was 6 or 7. Despite her age, Eliza was still active in the village and, for instance, was attending night classes in German.

The medical problem was that Eliza had been bitten on her lower leg by her cat, which she loved but the bite had caused a severe infection (cellulitis) of the whole of her lower leg and this was not responding to antibiotics prescribed by Dr Mary.

The only course of action was to admit Eliza for a course of intravenous antibiotics, but this was only possible after Dr Mary, Eliza and myself had made suitable arrangements for her cat. Eliza was admitted to one of my beds in a Nightingale ward of the old General Infirmary at Leeds and treated with intravenous antibiotics to which the infection responded well. However, she began to complain of indigestion, so in the days before endoscopy I arranged for a barium meal which showed Eliza to have a very large but benign gastric ulcer.

I went to tell Eliza of the result of the radiology feeling very positive because ulcers of this type would respond to appropriate medication from a drug derived from liquorice called carbenoxolone. This was in the days before stomach ulcers were shown to be caused by a bacterium known as helicobacter. I went to Eliza's bedside and told her we could heal the ulcer. To my surprise Eliza told me she was feeling very tired and said that she was not interested in having any more treatment. She turned her back on me as I spoke. I tried to encourage her by talking about her cat, her beautiful garden and the German night class lessons but all to no avail. Eliza just repeated that she was tired and that she had had enough. I went up to my office thinking that I had failed this woman, this nurse who had been a pillar of society in her village for so many years. Twenty minutes later my phone rang. It was the sister from Eliza's ward who told me that Eliza had just died peacefully.

Postscript:

People in some societies for instance, the Aboriginals in Australia, seem to be able to die when they wish but Eliza managed to die like this too.

I hope that I may be able to follow in Eliza's footsteps when the time comes. There is a lot of debate at present in the UK about assisted dying, suicide and euthanasia. Eliza showed me that sometimes we can do it ourselves.

SOME SAD SURGICAL STORIES

A Grateful Patient:

During our training as medical students, we were obliged to spend significant amounts of time being taught obstetrics and gynaecology. We were taught in small groups and the registrar deputed to teach us we found to be particularly aggressive, and our group were all relieved when he was promoted to be a senior registrar miles away from Newcastle in Workington a small town on the North West coast. After a period on obstetrics and gynaecology, each of our group had to arrange a three-month elective period during our final year. Three of us drew the short straw for Workington where we were exposed once more to this now senior registrar's lancinating tongue. As part of our elective, we had to watch and at times assist this man in theatre where it became apparent to us that he was not a born surgeon.

In my years spent as a medical student, and later as a junior doctor and consultant, I became convinced that there are relatively few born surgeons. Individuals who combine enormous dexterity with fine judgement particularly when and when not to operate are rare indeed. Much more common are surgeons who enjoy the drama of their work in a 'theatre'. These surgeons are good at creating theatre but lack dexterity. These practitioners aspire to be good surgeons but never quite 'butter the parsnips' and a lack of prowess is often compensated by a 'silver tongue' sometimes referred to as a good bedside manner. Finally, there are those, happily a small percentage, who should never undertake surgery at all. Operations go wrong, blood is everywhere, and wounds break down. These surgeons have a higher mortality and morbidity rate than their peers and from time to time throw surgical instruments about in theatre. Attempts at comparing surgical outcomes amongst specialist groups have gone some way towards identifying these individuals, but some even now, are slipping through the net and colleagues who have serious doubts about an individual surgeon's ability are reluctant to come forward to express their concerns to the relevant authorities. This particular senior registrar belonged, in my opinion, to the group who should never undertake surgery, but he had managed to progress to a senior registrar post one step below a consultant without any concerns being voiced. In Workington this individual operated on a young married woman whose first baby had died in utero late in pregnancy. On his own initiative, he decided to do a D & C (dilatation of the cervix and curettage) under general anaesthetic. The patient was very advanced in gestation and the uterus at this time is extremely vascular. The surgeon managed to put his curette through the patient's uterus and not only that but also through the wall of the adjacent large bowel leading to the development of a post-operative peritonitis. She became dangerously ill and was in danger losing her life from sepsis. Mr Arthur, a consultant from the teaching centre in Newcastle was summoned to Workington to try and repair the senior registrar's carnage. Mr Arthur was a religious man and after scrubbing up he prayed for five minutes or so in the corner of the little theatre. The woman's life was in the balance. Through an abdominal incision Mr Arthur washed out the peritoneal cavity which was full of foul-smelling faecal material and went on to repair as best he could both the colon and uterus. Post-op the woman had a very stormy recovery, and her parents and husband were at her bedside for days. For the next week or so it looked as if she would die from sepsis but eventually the antibiotics she had been given gained ascendancy and she slowly recovered. Both she and her family were immensely grateful to the medical team including the senior registrar. More than fifty years later I imagine the family are still grateful but the saddest thing about this was that the peritonitis so well established would make it impossible for the young woman to ever have a family. She had to cope with not only losing her baby but a later realisation that she could never get pregnant again. The senior registrar was subsequently appointed a consultant in obstetrics and gynaecology.

Postscript:

It is ironic that litigation often follows heroic attempts at doing the best for patients, whilst litigation never seems to follow horrendous mistakes such as this.

FURTHER SAD
SURGICAL STORIES

Mr X was a young Ear Nose and Throat consultant surgeon recently appointed to a Northern Teaching Hospital to run a Regional Laryngeal Cancer Unit. The idea behind this appointment was that the surgeon would operate on patients in conjunction with a plastic surgeon to rid the patient of their cancer from the voice box and also deal with any obvious local spread to lymph glands. A plastic surgeon would join the Ear Nose and Throat consultant in the surgery to try and ensure a reasonable cosmetic result following very radical surgery.

It was not long however before the plastic surgeon withdrew from the operating scene and the young Ear Nose and Throat surgeon continued to perform increasingly radical surgery on his patients, most of whom failed to survive after spending three or four weeks in abject misery post-operatively.

Concerns about the result of the surgery were becoming increasingly voiced amongst the nurses, one of whom began to collect data which showed survival rates approaching zero. Despite these concerns, operations continued until one day in theatre the surgeon had a grand-mal epileptic fit from which he recovered. Urgent investigations revealed a secondary frontal lobe brain tumour from a primary malignant melanoma. The surgeon followed his patients to the grave shortly afterwards.

Postscript:

The frontal lobe of the brain is important in influencing our behaviour and when its function is depressed, for instance by alcohol, or by a brain tumour disinhibition follows. A primary or a secondary tumour can grow quite large in the frontal lobe before symptoms occur and this was likely in this instance.

On balance, therefore, this brain tumour became responsible for the young surgeon's increasing lack of judgement.

ANOTHER WORRYING ENT STORY

An ENT Consultant working in a Northern Teaching Hospital visited Pakistan to give some lectures there to the country's ENT community. During this tour, the consultant was approached by a Pakistani consultant ENT surgeon asking if it would be possible for his son to come and train in the UK. The son apparently wanted to follow in his father's footsteps and the UK consultant acceded to his colleague's request and soon Dr Ali, a young man in his thirties began to tread the ENT wards in the North of England with an appointed rank of senior house officer. In his thirties he was, however, much older than most senior house officers who in those days were usually appointed one year after qualification and would be on average ten years younger.

The nurses soon had concerns about Dr Ali who did not seem to know what he was doing. One of the nurses alleged that he had an unusual habit of examining the tonsils via the female genital area! Anxieties about Dr Ali came to a head one night when he tried and repeatedly failed to take blood from a patient. After several attempts, which left the patient bruised, battered and sore on both arms, Dr Ali rang the resident medical officer (RMO) at about 3 am requesting assistance. Dr Ali was a bit unlucky as the RMO on duty that night was a rather fierce feminist who was not best pleased to be called out of her bed in the early hours of the morning to undertake a procedure any junior doctor, and indeed any clinical medical student, should have been able to accomplish with ease.

The RMO came and took the blood with steam coming out of her ears and told Dr Ali angrily "to put it on ice". In other words, put the sample in appropriate bottles in the fridge until the following morning. A little later Dr Ali was espied taking some ice cubes from the fridge and dropping the blood samples onto the ice using a needle from the syringe.

Postscript:

This was enough to have Dr Ali suspended on full pay but again demonstrates how difficult the medical profession finds it to 'rat' on a colleague until matters become extreme. No doubt the UK consultant surgeon was flattered by Dr Ali's father's request, but flattery is to be resisted.

There is considerable concern about medical degrees being handed out in the Middle East and Indian continent where numerous Medical Schools are being established with private money for financial gain and the General Medical Council (GMC) does not inspect these institutions. Photocopies of alleged qualifications should not be accepted by the HR department in hospitals and even an original document should be examined carefully for forgeries.

Although Dr Ali did not have any problems with alcohol, the alcoholic doctor is usually a subject of mirth until a medical disaster strikes, when they are 'kicked out of the tribe' unceremoniously. You are not expected to become mentally ill, alcoholic, depressed or anxious as a doctor as the stigma is too great. In reality it is alright to feel not alright, yet still many doctors fear loss of face if they join 'the other side as a patient'. Currently, anxiety and depression seem to be commonplace amongst medical practitioners and exacerbated by the Covid 19 pandemic. The abolition of the 'firm' the junior doctors mess and dining room and too many night shifts may be in some measure responsible.

ANOTHER SURGICAL TALE

In the UK, surveys have indicated that doctors are the most trusted professionals way above accountants, journalists, police and politicians. Public trust of doctors, however, is not universal, and I am told this is sometimes the case amongst the Chinese. Some time ago a wealthy businessman living in the UK developed indigestion and consulted a Chinese surgeon down that "street of shame" Harley Street in London. Following a history and examination, the Chinese surgeon advised an urgent endoscopy which was carried out the following day and subsequently the patient was told he had stomach cancer which had been confirmed by several biopsies and he would need an urgent operation to remove the whole of his stomach. The surgeon said he would carry out this operation in Hong Kong in about three months' time! The patient did not feel happy with this advice and consulted an old friend of his, a General Practitioner then working in Leeds Dr Roy Yeung. Roy graduated from Leeds Medical School but came from a well-known business family in Hong Kong where his grandmother was the first person to own a Rolls Royce. Roy arranged for the businessman to see a consultant colleague in Leeds and an endoscopy was carried out and biopsies taken. The endoscopy showed a perfectly normal stomach and not only that, the biopsies were all entirely normal. The gastroenterologist in Leeds wrote to the Chinese consultant in Harley Street asking for copies of the biopsy reports and surprisingly there was no reply despite several efforts to obtain these data.

Postscript:

The vast majority of doctors in the UK practise to the highest ethical standards but every year a handful are struck off by the GMC mostly for sexual offences, incompetence, drug abuse or fraud. Doctors are not immune to bribery particularly from the pharmaceutical industry and conflicts of interest abound. It has for instance been alleged that a UK pharmaceutical company, one of the largest in the world, went so far as providing prostitutes for doctors in China as an inducement to prescribe their drugs. The Dr Harold Shipman saga underlines the fact that care has to be taken in doctor/patient relationships.

Shipman, shortly after he qualified worked on a paediatric ward in Pontefract where it was alleged that an unexpected death occurred. Shortly afterwards Shipman was arraigned before the GMC for pethidine addiction, but in my view, he was probably using the pethidine to kill patients even then rather than taking it himself. Shipman was a very popular single-handed General Practitioner in the North of England and literally loved by some of his patients. His practice was audited shortly before he was arrested for murder and a glowing report ensued.

'Trust me I'm a doctor' is a phrase that needs treating with some caution. A healthy degree of scepticism is not amiss in these uncertain days.

JOAN OF ARC

After qualifying in 1963 and undertaking obligatory house jobs, I was unemployed briefly for the first and last time in my working life, I was obliged to sign on at the local Employment Exchange where discrimination forced me to join a clerical queue rather than a different queue allocated for the working class. After two weeks of signing on, I began to work as a locum GP waiting for a suitable hospital appointment to become available. I worked first in the wilds of Northumberland in a practice based in Rothbury, a very beautiful part of the world. The senior partner of the practice was a Doctor Armstrong, and his partner was Dr Bell. I was a locum for Dr Armstrong whom I believe was the grandfather of Alexander Armstrong a well-known radio and TV presenter. The pace was not too demanding, and the main challenge was finding farmhouses far off the beaten track especially at night. There were no mobile phones for communication in these days.

The 'biggest hitter' in Rothbury was Lord Armstrong who lived in his great Victorian pile 'Cragside' said to be the first stately home in the UK to have electricity. Dr Bell was not too enthusiastic about his Lordship whom he said resented paying seven shillings and sixpence (less than fifty pence) for a doctor's visit but happy to pay twenty guineas for a vet's visit to one of his racehorses. It was not surprising as a locum I was not invited to visit Cragside and see the noble Lord.

My next locum job was in Gateshead, a rough and tough lock-up practice. There were only two rooms, one for patients to wait in and one for me to see them. The patients would wait on the pavement outside until I arrived to unlock the waiting room. It was a single-handed practice and there was no receptionist, so I had to find all the notes myself. The practice itself dealt mainly with working class people and the elderly single-handed GP liked to take a holiday in Italy for six weeks each summer for which he arranged locum cover. Cunningly he also arranged all his on-call commitments with surrounding practices to his advantage and my great disadvantage. So, I found myself 'on-call' for most of Gateshead for two nights per week and most weekends.

Before he left for Italy this practitioner gave me the key to the front door and left with no explanation about the difficulties, I may encounter. I carried out a surgery each morning and each evening and carried out house visits in-between. There was always a crowd of potential patients outside on the pavement and a rush to get in first behind me. The room I worked in was dirty and ill-equipped. It was not sound-proofed, and I could hear the patients waiting to see me and I am sure they could hear me talking to the individual patients. The room was equipped with a telephone which started to ring as soon as I arrived, requesting home visits.

The battered bureau I worked at had one drawer containing loose phials of pethidine, a dangerous drug, which should always be kept under lock and key. There was always a large mail each workday. Most of the letters contained requests for repeat prescriptions for amphetamines with a stamped addressed envelope. Amphetamines were popular in the nineteen sixties and prescribed as an adjunct to weight reduction, but they were also popular on Tyneside as recreational drugs. I refused to prescribe on this sort of basis and would only prescribe amphetamines if indicated clinically, which almost they never were, when I saw the patient face to face.

One morning towards the end of a busy surgery I answered the phone. An anxious female voice explained she was worried about a lady next door, and I had better get round and see this woman as soon as possible. The line went dead before I could ask for more details. I finished the surgery as fast as I could and drove to the address given to me. I knocked at the front door and heard a key being turned in the lock. The door was flung open and there was a young woman dishevelled with long blonde hair dressed in a night dress (it was almost midday) brandishing a very large kitchen knife. "I am Joan of Arc" she declared. I felt strongly that we both needed help at that moment. She invited me into the house, and I went in with some trepidation. The woman clearly had an acute psychosis most likely due to schizophrenia and armed with a knife the most likely diagnosis was acute paranoid schizophrenia and I could easily become a victim.

I went back to the phone in the surgery and discovered finding a consultant psychiatrist in Gateshead during lunchtime was no easy task. The girl on the hospital switchboard was enormously helpful, however. No one was answering any of the clinic numbers she was dialling but after half an hour of this and eventually inspired she said "let's try the consultant's dining room". A very sympathetic and understanding Indian doctor came to the phone and courteously listened to my history without interruption. At the end of my diatribe, he agreed the woman needed emergency admission to a mental hospital for her own and society's protection. Thank God I thought. Then he said unfortunately he was not a consultant psychiatrist but a consultant in physical medicine so he could not help. However, he said there was psychiatrist in the dining room, and he would ask him to come to the phone. The whole process had taken more than an hour. Subsequently the patient was admitted under section and did well with appropriate treatment.

Postscript:

Medicine can be a dangerous business and GP's, dermatologists, plastic surgeons and psychiatrists are all at risk especially from the patients with acute paranoid schizophrenia and body image disorders. During my career I have had a large plant pot thrown at my head by a patient in casualty and avoided being knifed by a hospital in-patient who had become psychotic on large doses of steroids. It took three burly security men and me to control this man before I was able to tranquilise him.

TALES FROM THE MORTUARY

My next-door neighbour in Portugal is an affable loquacious twice married Bavarian of fifty something years called Franz. He and I have long chats, usually lubricated by beer, over the garden wall. Franz told me that his mother spent 16 years in a sanatorium because of tuberculosis and he was sent to England by his politician father at the early age of 14 to learn English which he speaks fluently and well apart from an inability to pronounce 'V' which he always expresses as a guttural 'W'.

Franz told me he was called up for National Service in the West German Army and his father made valiant attempts to get him out of this predicament using his many political connections but all to no avail.

After several delaying tactics Franz was forced to report to a Colonel in an army camp. The Colonel was very polite and let Franz explain at length why he would never make a good soldier. Franz told the Colonel he was hopeless at PE and had little or no stamina. Moreover, he found it difficult to get up early in the morning and his feet blistered very easily and so marching was out of the question. He added that he was a very nervous individual and had absolutely no killer instinct.

The Colonel listened attentively and told Franz that he agreed completely that he was unsuitable as a potential soldier. Franz warmed to this empathetic officer who told him that he should now report to another officer, a Major, at the end of the corridor. Franz found another charming, smiling army officer behind a large desk who was happy to confirm Franz was unsuitable for an ordinary military life and so for the next 18 months of his National Service he would be deployed as a mortuary attendant in a military hospital! Franz did his stint and wished most days he had been deployed as an ordinary foot soldier.

Some years ago, the pharmaceutical industry connived with mortuary attendants asking them to supply pituitary glands. The pituitary is a small gland at the base of the brain producing a wide range of hormones including growth hormone. At this time growth hormone could not be synthesised, and it was needed to treat youngsters who were failing to grow normally and for some genuine cases where there was pituitary gland failure. The mortuary attendants were paid for the little pituitary glands, but disaster resulted from this enterprising and presumably tax-free supplement to their basic salary.

The problem was that some of the pituitary glands removed contained an infectious agent capable of producing a fatal neurological disease in the recipient. This disease, Creutzfeldt-Jakob disease, had been recognised for some time as a feared but rare complication of working as a neurosurgeon, developing some years after a presumed accident with a needle whilst operating. The disease evolves rather like mad cow disease and leads to a slow lingering and horrible death.

Happily, growth hormone has now been synthesised and the use of this synthetic product to stimulate growth in children lacking growth hormone is absolutely safe.

Mortuaries are strange places and can be frightening especially at the dead of night when the slightest sound can be misinterpreted especially by the nervous. Whilst working as a medical registrar in Ipswich, I was asked by the casualty sister one night to certify a death in an ambulance. Ambulances of the 1960's were very ill-lit by a tiny twelve-volt bulb. Despite the lack of good light, I went into the ambulance and found a young woman flat on her back; she had no pulse, no heart sounds and her pupils were unreactive to light. There was no doubt she was dead, and I asked the ambulance driver to take the body to the hospital mortuary

Because the cause of her death was not immediately obvious, the Coroner's Officer was informed, and a Coroner's post-mortem was carried out in the mortuary two days later. I thought no more about the situation until I was phoned by the pathologist who told me the woman, who was in her early thirties, had been murdered. A stiletto of some sort had been used so the entry wound on her left flank was almost invisible. The stiletto had ruptured her spleen which is a very vascular organ, and she had bled to death internally.

I was in a bit of trouble with the Police who were not at all impressed with me and wanted to know why I had not discovered the murder when I examined the body in the ambulance. I explained I had no chance in the ill-lit ambulance and coupled with a near invisible entry wound to discover the cause of death and with reluctance the Police accepted this saying that the delay had almost certainly compromised their chances of apprehending the murderer.

However, the pathologist told me there was another problem. He had found recently deposited semen in the woman's vagina so someone in the mortuary had had sex recently with this female corpse. The prime suspect was the male mortuary technician who denied vigorously any involvement, but there was no DNA testing available in those days. What is interesting however, is that whoever had sex with the female corpse could not at that time be charged with any offence. It was not rape or assault as the victim was dead. Nowadays it is possible that the perpetrator could be charged with desecration of a body.

Many years later in the British Medical Journal was an account of a somewhat similar event in a Romanian mortuary. A young girl of nineteen had been admitted to the mortuary after being declared dead following a freshwater drowning. It is recognised that it can be difficult to establish death with certainty especially following a freshwater drowning so efforts at resuscitation are often carried out for longer in this situation. Incidentally, similar problems of establishing death occur following an overdose of one of the benzodiazepines with drugs such as diazepam.

The male mortuary attendant who had not much to do on that particular afternoon had sex with the girl and during this she came to life. God only knows what she felt at the time. Was she in hell? Subsequently the girl's family forgave the mortuary attendant as his perverted actions had clearly saved their daughter's life.

Some of us have the fear we may be buried or cremated alive. Setting up a bell for those buried was an attempt to allay such fears and led to the expression 'saved by the bell'. An old friend updating this for the twenty first century wants to be buried with his mobile phone fully charged.

Years ago, I worked as a locum for a Suffolk GP who had been bequeathed a beautiful Alvis car by a retired London surgeon in exchange for his radial arteries to be opened after he had been pronounced dead 'just to make sure'.

Sometimes very sad events were discussed in the post-mortem room. As a young medical registrar, I was asked to go urgently to the delivery room where a young woman had collapsed after giving birth to a normal healthy boy. The woman was a Swiss National in her early twenties married to an English vicar and this was her first child. The woman was unconscious, and I did a lumbar puncture. This contained blood so I suspected she may have had a sub-arachnoid haemorrhage, a type of brain haemorrhage, as a complication of her delivery. The woman died shortly after the lumbar puncture. Her husband was distraught and was left literally holding the baby. The following afternoon I was called down to the post-mortem room by the pathologist who found that the woman's brain had literally liquified. Why?

It was common practice in some maternity units to give a recently delivered mother an enema. Perhaps it was thought that this would help with the delivery of the placenta but there was little evidence that this procedure did any good. The Swiss mother had been delivered by a newly appointed midwife who had previously worked at The London Hospital, a famous teaching hospital in the East End. At this particular teaching hospital, it was apparently routine to give a newly delivered woman an enema using savlon diluted 1: 10,000 which was supplied by the hospital pharmacy to the maternity unit ready diluted. The new midwife decided to give the recently delivered woman an enema of savlon but sadly used the neat undiluted product which was avidly absorbed by the gut and went on to dissolve the patient's nervous system. This was a disaster and sadly an entirely preventable death. This was one of my most upsetting moments in the mortuary and I think the poor vicar must have asked God repeatedly why he allowed this to happen to his young and beautiful wife – a terrible test of his faith.

Postscript:

Horrendous tales continued to emerge from the mortuary, for instance relatives of an Indian man thought to have died following a road traffic accident, found him alive in the mortuary subsequently in November 2021.

The stories related above are eclipsed by the recent allegations that a NHS electrician had had sex with over 100 bodies in two South of England Hospital mortuaries, and moreover had videoed himself during some of these desecrations.

We live in an ever-increasing surveillance society and clearly there needs to be better surveillance for the dead. Perhaps it will be necessary for surveillance to reach the level now encountered by the rest of us still alive.

DREAMS

Many years ago, I was asked to give a lecture in French in Montpelier. My French was not terrific, but I was going to a French night class, and I wrote out my lecture in my best French and then asked my teacher, who was French, to check my work and correct what was necessary. Armed with this, my wife and I spent a few days with friends on the Costa Brava and then planned to drive to Montpelier. On my second night in Spain, I had a disturbing dream. In this dream I went to the lecture room to give my lecture but there was no lectern where I could place my notes and my host switched out the lights, so the room was in total darkness. There was no possibility of reading what I had written. I woke up sweating and agitated and although usually I cannot remember what I have dreamt, on this occasion I did, and I told my wife all about it.

We drove to Montpelier the following morning. The lecture was scheduled for seven pm. The weather in France was terrible with severe thunderstorms. The roads were dangerously flooded and eventually we reached our hotel. The weather was so bad that on that night thirty people were drowned in the neighbouring town of Nimes. My host asked me if I could delay talking until nine pm as people were finding difficulty to travel because of the floods and bad weather. I agreed. Eventually my host took me into the lecture room. There was no lectern, and the lights were turned out after he had introduced me, just as it was in my dream. However, I managed to get by in my less than perfect French.

Some years later after a lecture in Utrecht in Holland, I was invited to a dinner by my host and because I had spoken about emotional, psychological and psychiatric problems in dermatological patients, I was seated between two Dutch psychiatrists who lived together in Amsterdam. During our conversation, I told them about my dream and then the reality. The psychiatrists told me immediately that I had had what they termed an anticipatory dream and that one of them, Peter, had had a similar but much more upsetting experience.

Peter told me that he had had a vivid dream where he had driven to the hospital with his partner from Amsterdam to Utrecht and was parking in the hospital car park when he saw a girl in a red dress running across the parking area. She was being chased by an older man with a gun who then shot and killed the girl! Peter told me that he was so upset about the dream that he woke his partner up and told him how vivid it had been.

Sometime later Peter and his colleague drove to work in the normal way and whilst Peter was parking his car, a young woman in a red dress came running across the car park followed by an older man with a gun who shot and killed the girl! Apparently the man was Turkish and the girl his daughter and this was a so called 'honour killing'.

How is it possible to explain these anticipatory dreams and later reality? Psychiatrists seem to recognise this phenomenon but to me these events are totally inexplicable.

Some philosophers believe that there is no point in trying to understand the inexplicable. There is no doubt the human mind is very complex and may never be fully understood. The problem for doctors is that we have to deal with it every day. Herein lies the art of medicine.

BENEFITS OF A GRAMMAR SCHOOL EDUCATION?

I was a Sheffield Grammar School boy. At the age of twelve I decided to study Latin instead of German and everyone had to do French. Latin was expected at 'O' level for anybody wanting to study medicine in those days. In March 1955 the German master interrupted our Latin class to ask if any boy would like to take part in an exchange with an Austrian boy during the summer holidays. Apparently, there were not enough volunteers from the German classes and the total cost would be as much as £19!

I volunteered and in August of that year a boy from Vienna called Manfred, who was 15, the same age as myself, arrived to spend a month in the UK. At this time, we lived in a small semi-detached house which my father had bought new for £90 in the 1930's. It is amazing how things have changed. We had a new grey Austin A40 which was my father's pride and joy – until then post-war cars had been universally painted black. Times, however, were still austere after the war and even sweets were still rationed in 1955 but there was some light at the end of the tunnel.

Exchanges were organised by the Anglo-Austrian Society with the idea of improving Manfred's English and showing him Yorkshire at the same time. We visited the Yorkshire coast (Filey) where Manfred could not understand why on a hot summers day there was hardly anyone swimming in the sea. Manfred was a very good swimmer and dashed into the North Sea and learnt the hard way why no one was swimming as it was so cold. We also showed Manfred the Yorkshire Dales travelling in the

Austin A40 and staying in modest boarding houses overnight.

Then it was my turn to travel to Vienna accompanied by Manfred by train. The journey took 36 hours including a channel crossing and we arrived in Vienna on a summer evening to be met off the train by Manfred's parents who drove us to their large central city apartment in a brand new Plymouth convertible with a pale blue body and lots of chrome and cream leather upholstery. The apartment to me seemed to be massive and luxurious and there was even a resident maid to do the cleaning and some cooking.

The following morning Manfred asked me if I would like to play tennis. He explained he had to do some other jobs as he had been away for a month, but he had arranged a partner for me at the local tennis club. My partner beat me easily and I found out later he was the Austrian Foreign Minister's son. I was beginning to feel out of my depth. Vienna, like Berlin at that time, was a divided city with British, Russian, American and French zones. The city itself was in the Eastern Russian zone but whilst there was free movement between all the zones, care had to be exercised particularly in the Russian zone. For instance, you had to be careful about photography in the Russian zone if soldiers were around. Manfred's mother told me she was repeatedly raped by some Russian soldiers who were billeted in their apartment just after the war. The soldiers were Russian peasants who used the toilet to clean their food. Manfred's father, who was in the army during the war, later ran a large American company, 'The National Cash Registry Company' in Eastern Europe.

A few days after I arrived the American company president and his wife came to stay. They were both 'past their sell by dates,' but friendly and pleasant. I had never met an American before and the president's wife was bedecked in jewellery and described everything in Vienna and Austria as 'divine'. During dinner the president, whom I think in retrospect was mildly demented, said he only asked potential American employees two questions and if they answered correctly, they were hired.

He declared he was going to ask me these two questions after he learnt that I was an English Grammar school boy. The first question was 'what is one eleventh of one twelfth?' I replied quickly and apparently correctly. He then switched from maths to English and asked me 'what was a split infinitive?' I answered correctly explaining that a split infinitive happens when an adverb is placed between two parts of an English verb (to go boldly or to boldly go) the latter being a split infinitive. "You're hired" he exclaimed. As a grammar schoolboy, I was almost suffocated by English grammar and one cardinal sin in those far off days was to split an infinitive. Roy Jenkins, who wrote a very carefully crafted and researched encyclopaedic biography of Winston Churchill, claimed he found only one example of a split infinitive in the whole of Churchill's massive literary output.

Latterly English has come under massive attack from several quarters. The adverb itself is threatened. For instance, when premier league football clubs had English managers, adjectives were usually preferred to an adverb during an interview. On TV, so often, you heard the manager declare 'the boy done good'.

Management culture arrived in the UK at least in medicine in the early 1970's starting with a massive re-organisation overseen by Sir Keith Joseph, characterised by Private Eye as the 'Mad Monk'. Management at that time lacked a professional language and began to butcher the English language kidnapping good English words such as robust. Active became pro-active, problems not letters were addressed and usually not solved. Co-terminosity was the buzz word and nearly everyone in the NHS, and there were a lot of employees, had to communicate with every other employee. In Harrogate for instance where I did two clinics per week, the area gardener would write to me informing me of his holiday plans. One time I had a letter about a quadrantic template from management which I was unable to translate. I was informed that this was a new way of describing a four-bedded unit. Beside this sort of nonsense, you can always recognise any edict from a manager as it is always full of split infinitives. I am beware of and usually disregard any letter or notice containing plentiful split infinitives. The last assault on the English language is from Information Technology (IT) and texting in particular. Surely it is only a matter of time before novels are written in text modified language and I have already embarked on one. I am told that the bible is now available for IT text devotees.

But we digress from split infinitives. About ten years ago my wife grumbled that I never gave her any surprises – nice ones anyway. I arranged secretly for us both to travel to Munich over Christmas and New Year where my wife, who loved ballet and opera could watch some particular favourites of hers. We were going with a group of 'opera buffs' (which I am not), and the whole thing was arranged by a specialist travel agent. We were to fly to Munich in late December and as the date approached, I informed my wife about the surprise. She asked where we were going. I explained I could not tell her as it was a surprise. She asked whether it would be hot or cold? I replied cold. She declared she was not going! In the event, we arrived in Munich one cold and icy afternoon and the whole group were staying in a small central hotel near the Opera House. I was deputed to go out and buy some wine so that we could have a drink in our room before dinner. In the event we had two drinks of wine so arriving a little late for dinner. The dining room was not large, and all the seats were taken except for two seats at a table occupied by an elderly looking man and a younger woman. As we approached the two of them, they looked at us 'daggers drawn'. The atmosphere was icy but even so I asked politely if we could join them at the table. It did not take rocket science to detect the obvious reluctance but as there was nowhere else to sit grudgingly we were allowed to join them.

The atmosphere continued like the weather outside, very cold and icy. I tried a few niceties to break the ice and established the man was a headmaster of a well-known public school and had spent his life teaching English. Then my wife, to be polite expressed the opinion, that her husband had some idiosyncrasies about the English language such as split infinitives. In that moment Winter turned into Summer at the table. The headmaster began to speak passionately about the English language and the widespread adoption of split infinitives in particular. He could not abide split infinitives he explained. I told him of my experience in Vienna. After that we were invited to join the couple for every meal during our Munich stay, all courtesy of the split infinitive.

Postscript:

You will probably find many examples of split infinitives in my writings. It is no longer the cardinal sin it once was, so long as it is used in moderation. NHS Managers still have to learn what moderation means and so continue to rape the English language whilst at the same time creating mayhem, apparently effortlessly, in all directions.

SOME UNUSUAL PATIENTS

The Patient in a Cardboard Box:

She came to see me in outpatients in a large cardboard box. This was a woman of sixty-five referred by a weary colleague in Sheffield where investigations had shown possible, but very weak features of a disease called systemic lupus erythematosus, a condition known to make some sufferers allergic to light.

My patient was adamant but deluded she was allergic to light and so spent much of her day inside the box. Her husband had managed to drive her from Sheffield in the box but not only that, had also persuaded the porters to transport his wife to my clinic in the box. Her overlying fear was light. Her husband's overlying fear was his wife who was, in reality, phobic to light.

Sophisticated testing to ultraviolet light proved to me, and more importantly eventually the patient that she was not allergic to light. She did not have a true delusion but an over-valued idea and was able to accept, with some reluctance, and in time that she could emerge from the dark world of the box to normal life again.

Phobias are irrational and unrealistic fears – a fear of fear. Most of us have one or more phobias. I am not happy with snakes. Once after a lecture at Ayers Rock in Australia the host brought into the room a man with a large sack on his back. He tipped the contents onto the floor – twenty or more large snakes of various colours. The women in the audience screamed and stood on their chairs. Gradually however, the snakes became accepted by the audience and most people, including me, were able to pick up a snake. None were poisonous we were told later – it was just our hosts idea of joke.

Ann:

Ann was a schoolgirl of thirteen doted on and looked after by an aunt. The aunt almost smothered the child with a mixture of affection and ever-present concern and attention. Ann was almost suffocated by her aunt's well intentioned care. Ann was not really thriving either at school or physically. Although a teenager she was treated as though she was six or seven years old. Moreover, her aunt became convinced that Ann had developed 'the total allergy syndrome' a diagnosis invented by the Press.

Ann's food was being increasingly restricted because of this perceived allergy and she was losing weight

I spent hours trying to put the phobias and irrational fears to rest. I admitted Ann and much to her aunt's concern gave her a normal diet on which she thrived and put on weight. I carried out extensive validated allergy tests, mainly for the aunt's benefit which were all negative. At the time Allergy Clinics had sprung up in Yorkshire mostly operated by snake oil salesmen and people were being diagnosed with all sorts of crazy allergens. In addition, there was a general ignorance about true allergy, not only in patients but also in the medical profession. For example, one patient who consulted me, an educated and sophisticated woman in her fifties asked to be tested for allergy to Yorkshire, as her skin problem had only occurred after she had moved from Warwickshire to Yorkshire!

Nicola:

Nicola was an attractive middle-aged housewife with a huge medical problem – wart phobia. This began she told me on her honeymoon. As she and her husband were being rowed romantically to a little Greek Island, she saw the Greek oarsman had warts on his hands. That was the end of the honeymoon, and she had to go home immediately. Nicola would make an appointment for herself in my private consulting rooms when she felt she had a wart or warts that needed treatment. She would bring her own sterile dressing pack which she used to stand on after she had removed her tights which were always disposed of into the sterile pack and left for me to get rid of. She would indicate where she wanted liquid nitrogen applied and usually, I could detect no warts within the areas she indicated. I colluded therefore with her on her phobia. I would have to open all the doors on her way out as she was worried there may be wart virus on the handles. This problem was accompanied by suicidal ideation as her phobia made her feel very depressed and anxious. These feelings were only temporarily relieved by a visit to me.

Nicola's phobia came to a head when she took an overdose but survived. I referred her to a consultant psychiatrist, a colleague who saw his private patients on the same day as me in an adjoining consulting room. The psychiatrist thought that Nicola would benefit from hypnotherapy and suggested that this would be most relaxing for Nicola if he carried out the hypnosis in her home. Imagine Nicola's horror as she came out of the first trance finding the psychiatrist masturbating at her bedside.

This was a disaster and I felt guilty as I had referred Nicola to this maniac. Nicola told no one, including me, for some years. Who would believe a patient with profound psychological problems? It was only when other women came forward years later that the scale of the psychiatrist's abuse emerged.

He was arrested and charged but he walked into court bent almost double on a stick and his barrister provided medical evidence that he had dementia. Incidentally his wife was a psychogeriatrician. The court decided he was not fit to be tried but subsequently there was a trial of fact where his outrageous and criminal behaviour was established. In the event he evaded prison but was totally disgraced. Later another psychiatrist working in the same area was convicted and jailed for sexually abusing some of his female patients.

Postscript:

Medical students need some instruction about touching – when and how to touch at the bedside and during a consultation. Presently there are problems because of covid about shaking hands but hugging in the UK in the twenty first century is a definite NO NO. Simply taking the pulse can be reassuring to a patient. In these days of medical technology, there is so much potential diagnostic and therapeutic equipment between doctor and patient that a simple touch on the hands can be impossible. Personally, I would find such tactility very reassuring if I found myself, for example, in an Intensive Care Unit. Simple reassurance can be so important in patient management, but technically touching a patient without their consent can lead you being accused of assault.

Some societies are more tactile than others and for instance people in Southern Europe have different norms to those of us living in the colder Northern climes. In practice chaperones are becoming more and more necessary. Nicola's wart phobia precluded any skin contact with her at all.

Les:

I first met Les just before 2 pm at the start of my clinic on a very sunny early English summer's day. He was rolling about on a trolley and when he was not doing that, he would jump off the trolley and put his hands, arms and face under the clinic cold-water tap. It was difficult to get near him and he was wet through. Les told me that if he went into sunshine, his skin would immediately burn, but there was nothing to see on his skin on examination. Was he mad or did he have a real medical problem?

In fact, he had a very rare metabolic disorder called porphyria. Porphyrins are integral to the synthesis of haemoglobin, the red pigment present in red blood cells. In Les's disorder, there was a missing enzyme, so porphyrin metabolites built up in the body leading to a tremendous sensitivity to ultraviolet light.

In those days, we dermatologists had sun blockers but only with a skin protection factor of 2. This was disaster for Les as his job was a milkman which necessitated him working outdoors. His skin problem became worse, as his milk round progressed particularly on sunny days so he was in the habit of pouring cold milk from his milk bottles onto his 'burning' skin. This meant on a sunny day he had insufficient milk for his customers and as a result lost his business.

Postscript:

There are several different types of porphyria and not all are associated with light sensitivity. One type is thought to be associated with King George III's madness and is thought to have died out in the British royal family.

A Geordie Lad:

A young Geordie lad in his early twenties arrived in Casualty with a milk bottle stuck over the end of his erect penis. The neck of the bottle was restricting venous return from this organ, so it became massively and painfully enlarged. "How did it happen" he was asked. He replied, "the bottle fell off the mantlepiece"! The lad was anaesthetised, and the bottle removed in theatre; it had to be broken, a delicate task. Happily, his 'best bit' returned to normal proportions with no lasting sequelae. The lesson to be learnt from this is that you have to take great care when near the mantlepiece!

A Geordie Lass:

A Geordie Lass of 15 presented to Casualty with a very offensive vaginal discharge. The cause was not immediately apparent so an examination under general anaesthetic was arranged. The findings were amazing – 2 hairgrips and a rolled-up picture of Gregory Peck. These foreign bodies were removed, and the young girl made an uneventful recovery.

Margaret:

Margaret was a housewife in her fifties when I first met her. She told me she was born with a port wine stain on the left side of her neck, extending onto her left lower face. She covered the area with cosmetic camouflage very successfully, but it took her twenty or thirty minutes each morning to do this. Margaret told me that she was largely unaware of the port wine stain until she went to primary school where some of her class would tease her about it.

When she was about nine one of the teachers wanted to put on a tap-dancing display for the parents. Margaret loved tap dancing and became very good at it, so much so she was put in the front row of the dancers by her teacher. There was a dress rehearsal for the headmistress on the afternoon before the evening event. The headmistress said everything was fine 'but that' meaning Margaret had to dance on the back row because of the mark on her neck and face. Margaret told me she cried and began to feel different to all the other children in the school.

She saw a dermatologist but there was no effective treatment at that time. Laser treatment came many years later in the nineteen eighties and that is why she was referred to me. Margaret married. (It is interesting that most women even those with extensive port wine stains marry, whereas men with the same problem rarely do so). Margaret told me she was unable to have children and she and her husband decided to adopt. Margaret told me she was rejected as a suitable person to adopt a child because of her port wine stain. This began another sad period in Margaret's life.

In the early eighties I began to treat patients with port wine stains using a laser. I was one of the first dermatologists to undertake this work in the UK. I had visited Dr Apfelberg in Palo Alto in the States to learn how to use the Argon laser and later operated a pulsed dye laser kindly donated by Mr and Mrs Trust who raised money for this laser through their charity Laserfare. Margaret was referred to me at this stage and I began to treat her port wine stain which was extensive with the pulsed dye laser. The treatment was slow, but the results were good, and Margaret was very happy.

Halfway through her laser therapy Margaret was diagnosed with an overactive thyroid gland which failed to respond to either tablets or radioiodine therapy. At the time Margaret was getting thinner and thinner and more and more anxious due to her overactive thyroid. The only solution, she was told, was surgery, a partial thyroidectomy. Left untreated Margaret would die of her thyroid disease.

Margaret told me that she had decided against surgery. Why? I asked. Because she said the surgeon would have to remove her cosmetic camouflage and when she returned to the ward after the operation everyone would be able to see her port wine stain. I contacted the surgeon involved and explained Margaret's anxieties and eventually Margaret was reassured enough to have her surgery with a good result. She put on weight back to normal and I continued to treat her port wine stain which responded well.

Postscript:

Many patients with skin disease and especially visible skin disease such as port wine stain feel stigmatised – not without reason. Studies have been carried out for example, in a busy tube station in London when the space around a facial port wine sufferer was measured during rush hour. Individuals with port wine stains always had more space around them even in a crowd. Visible birthmark sufferers must feel this alienation underlying their fears that they are different. I have treated married women with port wine stains on their body for instance, who always undress in the dark and tell me their husband has never seen the stigmatising birthmark on their trunk.

Once my secretary sent an appointment for laser treatment to a patient after a GP request. The woman wrote to me complaining bitterly that the envelope contained an appointment with my hospital's address on it. Her husband who had never seen the port wine stain on her arm wanted to know why she was to attend hospital, and this upset her greatly.

About 60% of patients with a port wine stain can now be treated more or less satisfactorily but some laser treated patients do subsequently regress.

NORTH OF THE BORDER

As a consultant dermatologist I was asked quite often to prepare an expert report on a claimant's alleged skin problems. Occupational dermatitis was and still is a common problem accounting for very significant work loss nationally. In the bad old days, an expert was appointed not only for the claimant but also for the employer. The expert was expected to act like a 'hired gun' and litigation was expensive as two experts had to be paid. Latterly, Lord Woolfe proposed, there should just be one expert whose aim was not to be a 'hired gun' but whose report and evidence was solely to help the court. This change, it was hoped would save not only money but also time and should make it much easier for a judge to decide the case.

It was against this background that I was asked to prepare a medical report on a Scottish claimant alleging that his work at British Steel had caused him to develop skin disease. I sent the man an appointment, but his lawyers contacted me and said he was too ill to travel. Would I go to Glasgow to see the man there in view of his ill-health? This was an unusual request, and I could only recall one previous occasion where I had to travel to a patient's home. With some reluctance I agreed, but his lawyers contacted me to say that he was not well enough to be seen and could I arrange to see him in about a months' time. In the event I caught the 6 a.m. flight from Leeds/Bradford Airport arriving in Glasgow about an hour later. I had reserved a room in a local private hospital to see the claimant at 10 a.m. I had to kick my heels for more than two hours.

No one arrived at 10 a.m. I tried to ring his lawyers, but they had no idea where their client was. The claimant arrived just before 11 a.m. with no apology for his lateness. He was a man in his forties. I asked him to sit down and began trying to take a history. "Can you tell me when your skin problem began?" I asked politely. "Ye can fuck off" he replied. I tried again explaining I would need a detailed a history if I was to establish a causal link between his work and his skin problems so I tried again "Can you tell me what your work involved?" I asked. "Ye can fuck off" he replied. I tried again "Where are your skin problems?" I asked "Ye can fuck off" he replied not very helpfully.

I was obviously not going to get a history and I explained under the circumstances I could not proceed and began packing my briefcase. As I made for the door he asked "Aren't ye going to examine me?" I was very tempted to reply "You can fuck off" but resisted. "Okay I said" but he would only allow me to examine a small area of skin on his right arm. I explained I would have to examine all of his skin "Ye can fuck off" he said. The claimant had a small area of psoriasis on his right elbow.

I left and flew back to Leeds. I prepared a full report of my experiences with the claimant for the Scottish High Court in Edinburgh. The report faithfully contained all the claimant's expletives. I had never prepared a report such as this.

The case came to court, and I flew to Edinburgh for the hearing. I was the first witness and gave evidence in front of a Scottish Law Lord who could scarcely contain his mirth. The claimant worked for British Steel, and I concluded on the limited data available to me that his psoriasis on balance was not related to his work. I left the court, and the claimant was called next. I saw him striding down the corridor to court in a most confident manner. However, the hearing took a dramatic turn. British Steel, without any claimant knowledge had hired a private detective to investigate this man when he alleged, he was not fit enough to travel to Leeds. He was filmed getting onto a plane for Australia and spending three weeks in that country where he was also filmed partying every night. He lost his case!

Postscript:

In over thirty years as a consultant dermatologist, I have prepared over six hundred medicolegal reports. This report was like no other.

Many dermatologists are reluctant to undertake medicolegal work. I think the overwhelming reason is fear of having to give evidence in court. However, almost all cases are settled before court, 'often on the steps of the court' i.e. on the day before the hearing. Barristers like this manoeuvre as a settlement 'on the steps' means they can claim full fees for a day's work and go off to play golf.

REGINA – THE RED QUEEN: AN ICELANDIC SAGA

Regina was unlike any other senior house officer (SHO) I have ever worked with. A typical SHO would be in his or her mid to late twenties, a UK graduate planning a career in either general practice or hoping to specialise in dermatology. Moreover, almost all my SHO's over the years were unmarried.

Regina was very very different. She was a sixty something American lady who had trained as a medical student in the East German city of Leipzig – then part of communist East Germany. She was married to an English teacher called Cyril Pustan (her second husband) and the two of them had lived together in the communist paradise of East Germany. Regina was small in stature with grey hair almost down to her shoulders. Her face was sallow and wrinkled. She was, however, very zippy doing everything quickly and full of enthusiasm. At some stage she left East Germany and came to us in dermatology after a period working in casualty at Leeds General Infirmary. Whilst working in that department she acquired great acclaim for her ability to hypnotise. For instance, some of the nurses, technicians and doctors had been hypnotised successfully by Regina to stop smoking. She would also be called to help with hypnosis during difficult obstetric problems in the Leeds sister teaching hospital St James's. Within hours of starting to work in the skin department she hypnotised a room full of technicians, much to the irritation of their bosses as this interrupted 'vital research work'. I should add that I had no part in appointing Regina as an SHO in the department.

Whilst Regina was a most imposing hypnotist her Leipzig medical school training had failed to focus on other important issues such as examination. She had no idea for example how to do a rectal examination. At this time, I had a patient in the male ward with a history suggestive of an enlarged prostate gland, (frequency, difficulty and urgency). I asked Regina if she had done a rectal examination, she replied she hadn't as she had never been shown how to do it. Reluctantly I demonstrated the procedure after asking the man's permission. His prostate was indeed enlarged. I asked if Regina could repeat the procedure. He agreed, and she did, and then in a loud and rather excited voice declared she would practise the procedure on the whole male ward. You could sense immediately the anxiety of the other 29 male patients in the ward.

Regina extended her hypnotic expertise into dermatological therapy. One major problem were warts and these were often treated with liquid nitrogen which is rather painful especially for children. Dr Pustan would hypnotise potential patients, so for example if I counted slowly up to ten a child or adult patient would enter into a trance-like state. I could then attack the warts in a pain-free way with liquid nitrogen and reverse the trance by counting back from ten to zero.

One night Regina really showed her prowess. She had all the female patients (about thirty) placed in armchairs. Even in those days (early nineteen seventies) there was a good geriatric representation with a scattering of dementia not uncommon. Notwithstanding these problems Dr Pustan hypnotised the whole ward of female patients en masse, an amazing undertaking and just to prove it was no fluke she hypnotised the whole male ward a few days later.

So, we had an SHO who was not particularly cognisant of UK medicine but was a incredible hypnotist. About this time, I received two rather puzzling phone calls. The first from the orthopaedic department asked if it was alright to provide special surgical boots for Dr Pustan as she was going walking in Iceland. The second call, more troubling, came from a telephonist who told me Regina had an outstanding telephone bill of more than £1,200. At that time this was almost a yearly gross salary for an SHO. Where was she ringing, I asked? Iceland, they answered on a daily or more often basis.

I used to have lunch with Regina and the other junior staff in our own junior doctors dining room. There was usually some banter but Dr Pustan would always first make for part of the Daily Telegraph before she had anything to eat or join in the dining room chatter. I asked what she was reading? "Oh, she replied it is the commentary on a chess match in Iceland." To my complete astonishment she then told me she was the mother of Bobby Fischer who at this time had just started to play the Russian, Spassky in Reykjavik in Iceland.

It was a clash of two different political systems at the height of the cold war being fought out on a chess board in mid-Atlantic.

Dr Pustan then related a lot of details about her life and told me by the age of twelve her son Bobby could beat anyone in the USA at chess. However, when Bobby and his older sister were still in their teens and after Mr Fischer had 'left the nest' Regina told me, that for her, the most important thing in life was nuclear disarmament. As a result of this heartfelt belief, she left her children in New York to cope on their own and decided to go to Moscow. She related how she had sailed across the Atlantic and arrived in France only to be returned to the ship by French immigration officers. She told me she jumped off the ship at night, swam ashore and ultimately reached Moscow where she was photographed having tea with Mrs Khrushchev. By this time, she had left Mr Fischer for good and married Cyril Pustan.

In the American press Dr Pustan was usually referred to as the 'Red Queen' and was notorious for chaining herself to the White House railings. She also targeted Downing Street on one occasion and in a similar way at the Home Office.

The chess contest in Iceland proved to be very interesting in that Bobby was very difficult initially about the seating, camera and lighting arrangements. He insisted the three front rows for seated spectators had to be removed. He complained about the room seating and lighting and refused to play until all of this was altered, forfeiting the second match after losing the first after apparently making a simple error, Dr Kissinger, the most important political figure in President Nixon's administration, phoned Bobby twice to persuade him to play. On one occasion Kissinger explained he was ringing as the worst chess player in the world to the best chess player in the world and on another occasion exhorted Bobby to beat the 'commies'. In the event Bobby did return to the chess board but for the American political establishment, it was vital that capitalism should prevail.

Shortly afterwards Dr Pustan left the skin department for Iceland to join her son whilst he was initially engaged in the chess dual with Spassky. After she left, our department was invaded by the UK Press, but she had managed to evade them.

The third contest at Bobby's insistence was played in a small room usually used for table tennis and with no audience. And why was Spassky beaten so easily there?

The fourth and subsequent matches were played with an audience in the large auditorium, with front seating removed and cameras banned. Bobby subsequently beat Spassky very easily. Reports of the contest alleged repeatedly that Spassky was making moves as though he was hypnotised!! All I can say is that Bobby's mother was an incredible hypnotist and was in Iceland at the material time. Were all the arguments about seating and lighting to facilitate hypnosis in that room? Had Regina taught her son her hypnotic prowess or was Regina herself involved somehow in the contest? We shall never know about this, but we can speculate.

The Russians knew there had been some conjecture about the use of hypnosis in previous matches when Fischer faced Taimanov, Larsen and Petrosian. Moreover, the USSR Sports Committee considered Fischer may have been using hypnosis as early as the beginning of August 1971. Two psychiatrists were dispatched from the USSR to investigate whether the Americans were using psychological warfare and hypnosis in particular. Amazingly Fischer complained about the possibility of the KGB trying to hypnotise him during the match. There were further discussion of the possibility of Bobby using hypnosis and or telepathy during July and August 1972.

Postscript:

I am told after Iceland that both Bobby and his mother enjoyed a civic reception in New York. There was also discussion about a White House reception but in any event this did not occur. However, it was known that President Nixon followed Bobby's career very closely.

Subsequently, Regina turned up in Portugal as there was a revolution there and later, she went to Northern Ireland. Her postcard sent to me from Iceland featured a stamp with pictures of both Spassky and Fischer. Sadly I cannot find this memento and as an enthusiastic stamp collector I am mortified.

It is now known that Mr Fischer was not Bobby's father and that honour followed a brief encounter with a Hungarian who Regina met transiently before she married her first husband.

Sadly, Regina died in 1997 of cancer and Bobby also died in Iceland after spending some years in Japan. Bobby was ostracised by the US government in 1992 after he had played a chess match against Spassky in the then communist Yugoslavia contrary to US sanctions. He developed severe mental problems before his death.

A POTPOURRI OF EMPATHY AND CATHARSIS

Mary was a sixty five year old widow living in Beeston, not one of the most affluent areas of Leeds but well stocked with good, solid, honest Yorkshire folk.

Mary was referred because of severe and recurrent bouts of giant urticaria – swellings of the skin, lips, mouth, tongue and upper respiratory tract which necessitated several admissions to intensive care because of concerns about obstructed breathing. The condition had not responded to a variety of antihistamines and there was even a poor response to oral steroids. Moreover, all tests were negative.

Mary was becoming depressed about her ill-health and her doctors were worried because they were not controlling the situation. If quality of life is of paramount importance for happiness, then Mary had no quality of life, and her reactive depression was understandable.

I had an interest in the emotional and psychological aspects of dermatology, but Mary was always very defensive. She was a very private person, but I learnt she liked bingo. However, she had had to give up her bingo because of her severe medical problems. This led to a significant reduction in Mary's social life, becoming increasingly isolated and meeting with her friends far less often. I saw Mary frequently over a period of about two years, either as an out-patient or during one of her many admissions.

My penultimate out-patient meeting was unlike any of the other consultations. I asked Mary had she managed to go back to Bingo. Tears welled up in her eyes, her lips quivered ever so slightly, and she said "No" both tearfully and rather emphatically.

"You know" she said "bingo" but couldn't go on, my staff nurse offered tissues as Mary sobbed for two or three minutes. Then, between sobs, she said about two years ago she was going out to bingo when her husband said he had terrible indigestion. Mary explained she offered to stay with him, but he insisted she go to bingo which he knew she loved. When she returned home, she found her husband dead in the chair and the coroner's post-mortem confirmed death was due to a coronary thrombosis. By this time Mary was still crying, the staff nurse was crying, and I was crying trying to hold back my tears. We three slowly recovered and I asked to see Mary again in two months. Normally I would see her earlier following an emergency admission. There were no more emergency admissions. Mary came to see me symptom-free for the first time in two years and what's more she was playing bingo again and off all medication.

Postscript:

For two years Mary had bottled up her terrible guilty feelings over leaving her husband on that fateful night, but at last after she was able to express her emotions her skin problems totally cleared.

The consulting room is very important in medical practice and is increasingly under attack by information technology (IT). Often a computer becomes the centre of attention, not the patient. So much information can be gained on a one-to-one basis from the patient. For instance, how does the patient walk in? Do they have a confident stride? Are they bent and depressed? How do they sit in their chair, on the edge of the seat and anxious, or are they sitting back very relaxed? How are they dressed? How much eye contact is there? Or are there defensive responses like folding their arms following the doctors' questions. Do lips quiver? These non-verbal cues are often more important than what is said during the consultation. If the doctor is staring most of the time at the computer, all these valuable data are lost.

As far as empathy is concerned, it really is impossible to know what the patient is going through or thinking. I think it is alright to tell a patient this but to add "but I can try and understand what you are going through?"

Moreover, the doctor should not be afraid of showing emotion and if the consultation ends in tears, then so be it.

Erik:

I never met Erik and I do not know his real name, but this is his story.

I had been looking after members of a wealthy Jewish family for some years. Mr Greenberg (not his real name) was a businessman owning several large supermarkets. He had a wife Carol who was not Jewish, a son who had eczema and a daughter. His wife was blonde and beautiful, truly a trophy wife. The family lived in some style in a North Yorkshire village not far from Harrogate. Carol's daughter loved riding and her father had bought her horses so she could compete in show jumping and eventing. (Eventing involves show jumping, dressage and cross-country). The world seemed perfect for the family. The supermarkets were doing well and even her son's eczema was under good control.

I was surprised therefore, when Mr Greenberg consulted me accompanied by a young blonde American woman and a baby who had eczema. He said he was selling his supermarkets and moving to the States with his new partner and son.

Carol came to see me sometime later as an NHS patient. She told me tearfully her husband had not only left her for the States with his new younger woman, but also left her destitute. The large and grand house had to be sold as had all her daughter's horses. What's more Carol had to get herself a job working as a barmaid in a local pub in the village where she had formally lived so well. On the money she got from this job she managed to rent a tiny, terraced cottage, but most of her 'friends' and the 'friends' of her daughter had deserted them.

Carol not surprisingly was very depressed.

There was, however, one glimmer of hope for her daughter Judith. One older riding friend had stayed loyal and was taking part in a world championship show jumping event in Estepona on the Costa Del Sol. She invited Judith to go with her and said she would pay all the expenses. Carol was very excited for her daughter; the horses had been sent ahead and Judith and her friend were flying out to Malaga and hiring a car and then driving down to Estepona.

I saw Carol for follow up about a month later. This was an even more tearful consultation. Carol told me her daughter was dead – killed after a car accident in Spain. Carol told me, between sobs, Judith and her friend were driving south from Malaga towards Estepona when a car had veered across the road colliding head-on with the car driven by Judith's friend. Both Judith and her friend were gravely injured. An ambulance was called but it was allegedly only a private ambulance and without payment would not take the girls, who were unconscious, to hospital. Some time elapsed before a man drove up in a very smart sportscar. He asked what the problems were and said he would pay for the ambulance, which he did, and then drove off. The girls were then rushed to hospital but sadly Carol's daughter Judith died on-route, but her friend survived. Carol contacted her ex-husband telling him that his daughter had been killed but he refused to pay for Judith's body to be returned to the UK and at that time Carol had insufficient funds to bring her daughter home.

She asked the Spanish police, who were very sympathetic and helpful, if they could trace the man in the sports car so she could thank him for his kindness in paying for the ambulance. The Spanish police said they should be able to find the man fairly easily because he was driving, what they believed was a very expensive sports car. A few days later the Spanish police contacted Carol and said that they had found 'her man'. His name was Erik, and he was a former Rhodesian commando. He had left Southern Rhodesia when it became independent and worked later in the Middle East in security for an Arab sheik. Unfortunately, the Spanish police said he was wanted by Interpol for fraud. It was alleged he had defrauded the sheik of thousands of dollars. He had been arrested and was awaiting extradition to the UK. This was a double whammy for Carol who had to bear the guilt of having Erik arrested in addition to grieving for her daughter.

Carol came for follow up three months later and this was another tearful consultation. I asked what had happened. Carol told me Erik had been extradited to the UK, charged with fraud, convicted and sentenced to eight years in prison. He was presently serving his term in Wormwood Scrubs, an old and very rough prison in London. Carol said she had visited Erik and he was covered in bruises and had a black eye. Erik, although he was over six feet tall and strong, was being beaten up because he was a white man and ex-commando, by a group of Afro Caribbeans.

Carol went to see the prison governor and told him the story. He promised to get Erik to a more modern open prison and in due course Erik was transferred to an open prison in Yorkshire where Carol visited him on a regular basis, but still full of guilt about her part in causing his incarceration. After three years the possibility of parole presented itself and Erik was released and went to live with Carol in her little cottage. The inevitable happened; they fell in love. Life at last began to improve for them both.

About a year later Carol received a telephone call from a lawyer in New York to say her ex-husband had died and that he had left his whole estate to their son who was then living in York. Carol felt elated now that the family's financial problems would be solved. She phoned her son but he told her to "get lost", and that she would not get a penny from him. Elation turned to anger and despair.

Erik was particularly angry. As a young commando in Africa he had learnt how to make improvised explosive devices.

He constructed a bomb, took it to York and placed it on the son's doorstep where it exploded injuring but not killing the son. Subsequently Erik was arrested, charged with attempted murder, convicted and given a ten-year prison sentence. Carol committed suicide.

Postscript:

Erik in his Wakefield jail cell must reflect repeatedly on why he stopped at the accident all those years ago. If only he had not stopped, he would not be in prison for the second time. When the Spanish police detained him, he was about to take a car ferry to Morocco where he could have lived quietly out of the prying eyes of Interpol and happily for the rest of his life.

THE GAS MAN COMETH AND GOETH

I arrived for my afternoon clinic in Harrogate to find a note on my desk from my secretary requesting a domiciliary visit to a seventy-eight-year-old lady called Elsie. No more details other than an address and the GP's name were available to me. After a very busy clinic I felt quite tired and arrived on Elsie's doorstep at about 6pm. Elsie lived in a council house and there was a cat looking uneasy on the front doorstep. I knocked on the door and tried to go in, but the front door was locked. I heard a key turning in the lock and bolts being drawn and finally the door was flung open revealing an elderly lady with very untidy grey hair, two rotten grey front teeth and wearing a dirty apron. She demanded to know what I wanted, and I said her doctor had asked me to call. But then I smelt gas and I said to Elsie, "There is a strong smell of gas - I'd better come in and see what the problem is". "OK" Elsie replied. The cause was very evident. Elsie had put three pans on her gas cooker but had forgotten to light the gas. This was many years ago when town gas was not only very inflammable but also potentially lethal if inhaled. I went into the kitchen, turned off the three gas rings and flung open the windows not only in the kitchen but also in the two downstairs rooms. I said to Elsie "We'd better go outside for a while,' whilst the house was ventilated.

After about fifteen minutes we went back into the house and then I said to Elsie "Let me have a look at your skin." She replied, "She wasn't going to take her clothes off for any gasman." She was adamant about this, and I failed totally to examine her.

Postscript:

Dementia is an increasingly common problem in our ever-aging population, and it is sometimes difficult to recognise. Elsie's presentation was, potentially lethal. She lived alone and her GP had failed to recognise her evident dementia.

When I was a young locum GP I used to visit elderly patients on a regular basis and I think this was the custom many years ago but less often now. Evidently GPs have increasing pressures on their time and regular surveillance is becoming increasingly rare, although the possibility of utilising IT is being investigated. Care however has become centralised around the surgery. Nurse practitioners specially trained in the care of the elderly may be one solution, but the problem is always continuity of care. True family medicine barely exists anymore. As a potential patient over eighty years old, I have been given a designated GP but have only seen him once. On my other visits I have been seen by one of several partners or by nurses. In the good or bad old days, depending on your point of view, the GP would bring you into the world and he or she would come to know the family intimately. Nowadays lack of GPs and severe deficiencies in social care are imposing almost impossible and increasing problems on Hospitals, Accident and Emergency Departments and Care Homes – exacerbated by the present covid pandemic.

Robert:

Robert was a patient of mine for many years and worked as a tea-taster/blender and although he was only in his early fifties, he looked at least twenty years older because he had a rare scarring disease called systemic sclerosis. This progressive scarring disorder potentially affects almost all parts of the body, but in Robert's case it was predominantly affecting the circulation to his skin and fingers in particular. He had suffered from this disease, (for which there is no cure,) for 25 years. During this time the circulation to his fingers had gradually become compromised necessitating surgical amputation, first the finger ends and then the whole finger one by one.

Robert loved his job which was highly skilled, but his ability to lift cups of tea to his mouth became increasingly compromised. Not only was he losing his fingers, but he was in a lot of pain because of the reduced blood supply to his hands, causing very indolent and painful ulcers at the ends of his fingers necessitating further surgery.

For Robert there was less and less light at the end of the tunnel. He had to give up his job which he loved. Robert told me during his last visit to my clinic that life was not worth living and shortly afterwards he took his own life.

Postscript:

Cynics, usually colleagues from other medical and surgical specialties like to tease dermatologists with the jibe that their patient's never get better and never die so it is thought to be good for private practice. Robert illustrates that skin disease may affect the quality of life so badly that resulting reactive depression can lead to suicide.

Every potential health care worker and particularly dermatologists should watch the TV play 'The Singing Detective' by Dennis Potter – himself a long-standing sufferer of psoriasis. I think he saw most consultant dermatologists in the UK except myself. The mental and physical agony of generalised psoriasis is portrayed magnificently by Potter in this play. Doctors, when faced by incurable diseases, must work and help the patient to accept the situation. Failure of acceptance leads to hostility, anger and sometimes self-harm.

If you are condemned to a wheelchair, you can either smile or scowl. You may as well smile and accept the burden even if this involves some incongruity of affect. The battle Stephen Hawking had with his muscle disease is an example of a long-standing self-coping mechanism.

One of the many problems doctors face is that investigative medicine is more advanced when compared to effective therapeutic medicine. Managing a patient with incurable disease is a challenge to both patient and doctor alike.

ANATOMY DEMONSTRATORS

In the first pre-clinical year at Medical School dissection was an important part of anatomy teaching. Initially six medical students were allocated to each body. Three would dissect on one side and three on the other. Single organs would be shared. To help us, some anatomy demonstrators were deployed by the anatomy department, and we were all given an oral examination over the body every week or so by these gentlemen. The demonstrators were recently qualified doctors who wanted to become surgeons. To this end they had to pass the first part of their FRCS (Fellowship of the Royal College of Surgeons) with a heavy emphasis on anatomy. Their time in the dissection room was thought to be a good grounding for embryo surgeons.

Medicine is a broad canvas enabling most aspirations to be filled. Four demonstrators come to mind in this regard. There was Anthony Grabham (later Sir Anthony Grabham) who became not only a distinguished surgeon but a potent medical politician, well respected by Barbara Castle the Minister of Health at the time. Mrs Castle had proposed shutting down all the private beds in the National Health Service, so ending, she thought, private practice in the UK. To be truthful there was always some resentment about private patients in National Health Service Hospitals, but the private patients were paying and expected icing on the cake whilst being cared for by an 'off-time' understaffed NHS ward. The private patients were usually nursed in cubicles which was rarely necessary from a nursing point of view, whilst the NHS patients who could benefit from cubicle care were having to be nursed on the ward. Some larger hospitals had dedicated private wards, but Mrs

Castle wanted to clear these beds too and make them available to NHS patients. Tony Grabham fought his corner but many of the private beds were closed. The irony of this was that Mrs Castle, a labour politician, gave the biggest stimulus possible to private practice in the UK. The closure of the private beds led to the building of numerous private hospitals by BUPA, the Nuffield foundation and others and private practice continues to thrive as a result to this day.

Dr McStay was another demonstrator, tall, blonde, blue-eyed and handsome. He was nick-named by the male students 'Gods gift to women', I suspect the motivation was jealousy. He went on to become chief medical officer during the construction of the Tyne Tunnel which was dug out under the river Tyne using compressed air to prevent any flooding from the river above. The compressed air working environment led to the potential problem of bends, the same situation seen in deep-sea-divers. This decompression sickness was caused by a too rapid return from high to normal pressure. This is just like when a bottle of champagne is opened, a lot of bubbles are generated so the same thing can happen in the blood stream, blocking the arterial supply to bones, brain and other organs - a real medical emergency.

Dr Hedley Brown went on to marry a girl from our year and became a distinguished heart surgeon. In his spare time, he also built his own aeroplane which was licensed to fly but he only flew it once!

Dr Paul Vickers was more reserved than the other demonstrators. He went on to become a consultant orthopaedic surgeon in Gateshead. I am told he also served on the British Medical Association ethical committee but this could be fake news.

Vickers had a wife who was said to have mental problems probably schizophrenia. He also had a girlfriend who was Mr Heseltine's – later Lord Heseltine's secretary. Vickers had a proclivity for tea dances which were held on a regular basis in the centre of Newcastle. At this time Vicker's wife began to develop episodes of bone marrow failure. All elements produced by the bone marrow became depressed and she was admitted repeatedly for investigation and blood transfusions. However, her bone marrow seemed to recover well in hospital but soon relapsed when she returned home. In the end however, she sadly died. Vicker's girlfriend was apparently upset by Vicker's devotion to the tea dances and other women rather than her and so she went to the police to say she collected a regular prescription written by Vickers from the chemist for a toxic drug Methotrexate, a known bone marrow suppressant. Vickers was arrested, charged with murder, convicted and sentenced to thirty years in jail. His girlfriend was not charged or convicted as she had revealed all she knew to the police.

Postscript:

Medicine is indeed a broad church as the careers of the four anatomy demonstrators show. Some years later during a year reunion, Graham Teasdale (later Sir Graham Teasdale, Professor of neurosurgery at Glasgow University) recollected an article by Vickers published in our medical student's Gazette, when he was a medical student. The article was on poisoning!

CAT FLEAS

In 1973 I bought a larger house for my family after I had been appointed a consultant dermatologist in Leeds. The previous owners had bred cats and although my wife scrubbed all the floors, (I am constantly reminded of this) we were to experience severe problems during the hot summer of 1976 with cat fleas.

On the day in question, I came downstairs for breakfast and there seemed to be a haze in the dining room. This was due to thousands of cat fleas jumping up into the air from the carpet. My wife took one look and said she was off to her sister's in Newcastle with the children and that I could ring her when I had sorted out the problem. There was an epidemic of cat fleas that year, but the experts were not offering any certain solutions. However, I bought six cans of fly spray and emptied five into the dining room concentrating on the carpet. I presume the fleas were being generated from eggs still present under the carpet and in the gaps of the floor boards resulting from the previous owners hobby of breading cats.

I had had a busy day which culminated in a request for a domiciliary visit to a patient north of Ripon. After this domiciliary visit I had a good meal washed down by a beer at Da Mario's a restaurant on the banks of the River Nidd in Knaresborough and a favourite eating place for myself, my wife and our children. I then drove home, feeling very weary. I went into the dining room and all seemed quiet, so far so good I thought. I enjoyed another beer, watched the news on TV and went to bed.

I was awoken in the early hours of the morning by an intense itching on one of my legs. I put on the light, and I had been bitten in several places. There must be cat fleas in my bed

I concluded, half asleep and half awake. I pulled back the bed linen but could see nothing. I went back to sleep, dozing lightly because of the itchy leg. I was then bitten again. I was so cross and half asleep I sprayed the whole of the remaining can of fly spray between the sheets. That would fix the problem I thought and dozed off.

Less than twenty minutes later I woke up in left heart failure manifest by severe breathlessness and a strong feeling I was going to die. I crawled to the window and opened it gasping for breath. Happily, I had the wit to take a shower to wash the fly spray off my skin and I recovered over the next half hour. That would have been a good one for the Coroner I mused.

Postscript:

The skin is the largest body organ, and many chemicals can be absorbed by the skin. It appeared I had absorbed toxic amounts of fly spray under the occlusive effect of the sheets. The cat fleas had truly had their revenge.

THE GLOVED HAND

The first meeting of the European Society for Dermatology and Psychiatry was held in Vienna. It was organised by Professor Peter Berner, then professor of psychiatry in Vienna and delegates, mostly dermatologists and psychiatrists, psychologists and psychotherapists came from all over the world, but mostly from Europe, to the meeting.

There were some early frictions between delegates and in particular between psychotherapists and psychiatrists. Moreover, some Jewish members of the Society elected to stay away because Kurt Waldheim was Austrian Chancellor at the time and his murky past in the SS during the Second World War had recently been revealed. Incidentally, the term 'Waldheim Syndrome' was coined to describe individuals with a selective amnesia for events occurring between 1939 and 1945!

In my welcome I tried to ease some of this antipathy by pointing out that there are many ways of cooking an egg and we should all be tolerant of each other in our united quest to help patients.

The meeting attracted some colourful participants. All attendees were subjected to a lunchtime of laughter therapy by a Dutch practitioner. We spent the best part of an hour in a lecture theatre laughing at nothing, but laughter did prove somewhat infectious. However, I felt no immediate or later benefit.

One of the participants a Danish psychiatrist told the meeting that he was a world authority on self-mutilation. He wore a leather glove on his left hand and there was much speculation about what lay under the glove. In Vienna he seemed to have some problems balancing and the overall opinion of the kindly delegates was that he had some sort of neurological problem, perhaps even a peripheral neuropathy, when nerves in the hands, feet and limbs failed to work properly.

The next meeting was held during the summer in Leeds two years later, and participants were housed in one of the university halls of residence normally occupied by students during term time. The meeting was well attended and the Danish psychiatrist with the gloved hand registered once more. He was, however, accompanied by a younger Danish woman and he insisted that the two of them should be given adjacent rooms. I was tolerant and understanding so this was arranged, and he would go on to deliver a further paper on self-mutilation when the meeting got underway the following day. However, on the first night there was a reception where alcohol flowed and the following morning an Irish group of dermatologists asked to move, as two delegates in their corridor were very noisy into the small hours. The two delegates in questions were the Danish world expert on self-mutilation and his girlfriend. The following day was hot and sunny, rather unusual for an English summer's day. Jackets and ties were abandoned, and windows were thrown open. I was on duty at the registration desk when the Danish doctor rushed up and said he was furious that his lecture had been terminated early by the chairman when he was only halfway through. He was going to report the whole incident to the Danish Medical Research Council. His breath smelt strongly of alcohol and his gait was very unsteady.

During the morning break for coffee the chairman of the Dane's session, the professor of psychiatry in Leeds, came to see me. He said the session had taken a very bizarre twist. Whilst the Danish world expert on self-mutilation was talking, a car alarm went off in the adjacent car park. This was falsely interpreted by the drunken Dane as notice by the chairman that his time was up and so he walked out of the lecture angrily halfway through his presentation.

We shall never know what was under the glove. Perhaps the covered left hand was a victim of self-mutilation. Perhaps it was gloved to prevent further self-mutilation. Perhaps the hand was relatively anaesthetic because of an alcohol induced peripheral neuropathy

Postscript:

Alcohol can be a problem for some doctors. As a medical student all social events, and there were many, were almost always sponsored by the drug industry or insurance companies, and massively lubricated by alcohol.

Once qualified it was not unusual for alcohol and beer in particular to be delivered to the hospital mess free of charge. Mess parties and mess dinners were never short of alcohol. Conferences and medical dinners were never dry.

Add to all this cocktail, the fact that a life in medicine can be very stressful and alcohol is a good but very short-term reliever of stress. The role of alcohol as a social facilitator has to be balanced against the potential problems of long-term abuse which includes cirrhosis of the liver and some cancers (liver and oropharyngeal) heart irregularities (atrial fibrillation), alcoholic dementia and the potential for self-harm after falls amongst others.

LIQUORICE ALL-SORTS

The professor of medicine in my early days in Leeds, was an eminent medical politician being on most important medical committees in the UK and even more. In his absence his work was carried out by a small army of National Health Service and university employed deputies. One of the duties of juniors was to try and keep experts like professors of medicine away from patients nominally under their care, as all the committee work they undertook could have a serious deleterious effect on both their medical knowledge and abilities.

During a rare ward round the professor came across a patient under his care with extensive vitiligo. Vitiligo is a condition characterised by the development of white areas of depigmented skin commonly on visible areas such as the face. The professor asked his staff to get a dermatological opinion as he hadn't a clue what the problem was and some days later, I went to see the patient. The delay was not on my account because the request for a dermatological consultation, thought to be relatively unimportant, had taken some time to arrive in my department.

I found a woman in her fifties with extensive vitiligo but more importantly she was near to collapse with a very low blood pressure. This was because she had a disease known to be associated with vitiligo and characterised by failure of the adrenal glands which secrete the hormones cortisol and aldosterone. In short, she had Addison's disease. These hormones are necessary to deal with stress and maintain a normal blood pressure. Without treatment patients with Addison's disease can go eventually into a crisis which can be fatal due to lack of these essential hormones. A hydrocortisone drip is curative in the short term, and I took over her care and she recovered well with this.

As a medical registrar years ago in Ipswich I was taught that patients with Addison's disease sometimes become addicted to increasing amounts of liquorice. Liquorice contains a chemical that, as long as there is some adrenal gland activity, will help the body retain sodium and water essential in normal homeostasis and therefore in blood pressure control. However, I had never been able to find any reference in the medical literature to this. I asked my patient if she had been eating liquorice and she replied "Yes". During the last two months she had developed an increasing taste for Bassett's Liquorice Allsorts and was regularly consuming three quarters of a pound per day. She felt a lot better after liquorice ingestion but more recently found that the liquorice was not helping her so well and since she was admitted to the ward she had had no access to Liquorice Allsorts.

I wrote a small paper on this association which was published in the Lancet and a week or two later there was scathing letter from a London chemical pathologist a Dr Nabarro, I think possibly a brother of Sir Gerald Nabarro, then a well-known Tory MP. Dr Nabarro scalded me for not reading the literature properly and had I done so I would have found the association had already been reported by Dr Richard Asher a very distinguished physician working at the Central Middlesex Hospital and most famously father of Jane Asher, friend of the Beatles and later an actress of great talent.

Dr Richard Asher made many important contributions to the medical literature and believed in calling a spade a spade and railed strongly against any complicated medical terminology. Therefore, I was amazed to learn from Dr Nabarro that Dr Asher had described liquorice addiction in a patient with Addison's disease under the heading of "glycerorhizophilia". What chance had I or anyone else of finding this association in the medical literature?

Postscript:

Stories abound about Dr Asher. He was loved by his patients and students alike but was at war with his medical peers and the hospital administration. He had a particular interest in the psychological presentations of general medical conditions and put myxoedema (hypothyroidism) madness on the map. He wrote about the danger of putting patients to bed, of complications such as deep venous thrombosis and bed sores in particular. He described a very unusual gait in his daughter Jane, when a little girl, only to discover that he had placed both of Jane's legs down one knicker hole whilst dressing her. Another major contribution of his was to describe patients with Munchausen syndrome who set out to fool the doctors by all manner of contrived but non existent diseases.

He was a man of great kindness and compassion and liked to give his patients presents at Christmas and would ask what they would like. I was told that one Christmas he was looking after a twelve-year-old girl who was dying of leukaemia, and she asked if he could bring the Beatles to her bedside which he did, because his daughter Jane was friendly with the Beatles at the time.

Students loved Asher. He would give an annual lecture on how not to give a lecture appearing with his fly zip open and part of his shirt hanging out. One student was instructed to beat a drum at the back of the lecture theatre during the whole of the performance. The slides were arranged chaotically. Pictures of the female vulva were always upside down, normally a sure indication of a new female projectionist. He famously taught on a patient with narcolepsy, a neurological condition where the patient lapses into unconsciousness when excited. Asher's patient was a keen fisherman and used to lose consciousness when he got a bite. Often, he fell into the river and had to be rescued by adjacent fishermen.

Asher's war with the medical establishment left him increasingly isolated, he developed a duodenal ulcer and sadly later committed suicide.

Asher railed against complicated medical terminology and this is underlined by the quote by Dr Asher, "Well I ask you? When you take your family on holiday, do you say 'I am taking my gregarious, egalitarian sibling group with me?' This was written by Richard Asher in 1959 and it seems completely out of character that he should introduce a new term into the medical literature of Glycerorhizophilia.

The medical history of liquorice is interesting. It is said that the Arabs crossing the desert would chew liquorice in an attempt to retain body fluid. More recently the drug carbenoxolone derived from liquorice was shown to heal giant benign gastric ulcers.

The manufacturers of Bassetts Liquorice Allsorts heard of my Lancet paper and sent me a large box of Allsorts. My daughters had a very pleasant birthday.

Addison's disease can be a very difficult condition to diagnose as the presenting features are often non-specific including fatigue, weakness, lethargy and depression. One unusual patient reported in the literature would experience episodes of anxiety, palpitations, panic, light-headedness, and a sense of impending doom towards the end of a high-profile football match when Manchester United was playing. Similar symptoms occurred during matches between Manchester City and Chelsea where sometimes the outcome of the match was in question until the last minutes. The endocrinologist looking after this patient believed that she was having difficulty producing cortisol in sufficient amounts during the big games and concluded that the patient had a Manchester United induced Addisonian crisis. With appropriate therapy her symptoms disappeared during subsequent football matches.

On the other hand, a liquorice habit is known to have caused at least one patient's death. In the States a fifty-four-year-old man had a cardiac arrest caused by glycyrrhizic acid, the active ingredient in liquorice. The patient got into the habit of eating a pack and a half every day for at least three weeks prior to his demise. It is known that glycyrrhizic acid can cause high blood pressure and low blood potassium, fatal heart arrythmias and renal failure.

Like my daughters, I love Liquorice Allsorts but it is important to be governed by the saying 'everything in moderation'.

OLD MOULDY

When I arrived in the Skin Department in Leeds in 1969 Dr Charles La Touche (Old Mouldy) was the dermatological mycologist, an expert in fungal disease and in fungal disease of the skin. It would be an understatement to assert that 'Old Mouldy' was somewhat eccentric. He would arrive in the skin department well after 9 am and mash himself a pint of strong tea which seemed to have a cathartic effect on his bowels which he would then open and after that he was open for business in his laboratory. There was no possibility of communication before 'Mafeking' was relieved.

'Old Mouldy- was said to have an Irish medical degree and some doubters expressed the opinion that he may have paid fifty guineas to a man in a jogging cart for this degree, but I am sure that was fake news.

'Old Mouldy's' first job was at a research institute linked to St Mary's Hospital in London. His laboratory was one floor under the laboratory of the then Professor of Bacteriology who was in the habit of leaving his culture plates on his windowsill to see what evolved. One day in 1929 the Professor (Alexander Fleming) saw an area of lysis, indicating something was killing the bacteria, on the culture plate. 'Old Mouldy' identified this fungus as a penicillium mould and this simple observation and discovery led to the development of penicillin and many more antibiotics subsequently.

It is pure conjecture, but it is thought that the penicillium mould originated from 'Old Mouldy's' laboratory and in this regard, I have to say that 'Old Mouldy's' laboratory in the skin department at Leeds General Infirmary was not particularly pristine in terms of cleanliness. However, many important medical discoveries have been made by chance and this was, happily for humanity, the likely case here.

Scalp ringworm used to be a terrible problem especially in school children. It was very infectious and infected children were kept away from school. There was no ready cure and x-rays were used to destroy the hair follicles on the scalp and therefore the infected hair roots. The problem was that there was a very narrow window between effective depilation and serious radiation induced side effects such as skin and bone necrosis which resulted in infection and even blindness. Extensive skin grafting was sometimes necessary and there were consequences many years later such as bone and brain tumours. Most older dermatologists would have to look after two or more children who suffered these consequences after x-ray therapy, and it was a nightmare therapeutic situation until the antifungal antibiotic griseofulvin became available in the nineteen fifties. About one thousand five hundred antibiotics have now been discovered although not all are suitable for human use and possibly none of these would have evolved but for the discovery of penicillin where 'Old Mouldy' played his part.

'Old Mouldy' decided to retire in the early 1970's. Deciding to take up art on his retirement, the department bought him a good set of oil paints. During his retirement presentation someone told a story about 'Old Mouldy' which went something like this: There was a society called the North of England Dermatological Society (NEDS) and there was always an annual dinner in Manchester at the Midland Hotel after a prior clinical meeting of the Society in the Skin Hospital. A group of doctors including 'Old Mouldy' attended this meeting and a good dinner was had by all. This was in the days before the breathalyser and before the construction of the M62. After the dinner the group set off back to Leeds in one of the consultant's (Dr Steven Anning's) Bentley. Steve Anning was one of the three Leeds consultants and enjoyed all the fine things in life. The journey took more than two hours in those days and involved navigating twisting roads and transit through endless villages and towns. It was a dirty dark night and raining heavily. As the Bentley was climbing over the Pennines in the middle of Saddleworth Moor 'Old Mouldy' said he felt sick. Steve Anning stopped the car: 'Old Mouldy' got out and vomited over a small wall no more than two feet high. After that he declared he felt much better, but it was never clear whether he had been car sick, or he had had too much to drink at the dinner. In any event 'Old Mouldy' then declared he had lost his teeth. The other occupants of the car were well oiled but felt well-disposed to solving the problem and jumped over the little wall hoping to find 'Old Mouldy's' false teeth. All to no avail. There was a considerable drop on the other side of the wall, and they all landed in a wet heap of vomit. 'Old Mouldy's' teeth were claimed by Saddleworth Moor where I suppose they remain to this day.

'Old Mouldy' was succeeded by Dr Glynn Evans, a young Welshman. Our families were of a similar age, I used to take my three girls and Glynn took his two sons to Leeds/Bradford Airport each Sunday in the late morning. In those days you could park easily at the Airport for nothing, and the children could run around whilst we had a pre-lunch beer.

We planned when we both retired to try and grow the truffle fungus in the laboratory. Sadly, before we could do this Glynn died and meanwhile a Japanese team grew a truffle fungus artificially. However, it tasted horrible, and I forgot all about truffles for several years.

Later when I was retired, I saw an advert in the Financial Times for land in Tuscany suitable for a truffle farm. I took my wife out to look at this land and she declared she was one hundred per cent against the project, so I knew immediately: I had to do it -create a truffle farm in Italy. The farm is now ten years old and produces some black winter truffles each year. However, because of the Covid 19 pandemic I have been unable to visit the truffle farm for over eighteen months. I am not quite sure what I shall find, if and when I manage to get there.

WILMA AND KLAUS

Many years ago, I was invited to give a lecture on psychiatric problems in dermatology by the Swedish Dermatological Society. The meeting was held in Uppsala and two other speakers were also invited. Wilma from the USA and Klaus from Austria. At the time Professor Klaus Wolf was one of the most outstanding European dermatologists and had even a stamp with his face on issued by the Austrian Post Office. Wilma also had a similar worldwide reputation. These were two very heavy 'hitters' and I felt a bit like a fish out of water. The three of us met together in an ante-room adjacent to the lecture theatre. Wilma noted that Klaus had an identical gold Rolex watch to hers and it soon transpired that the watches had come from the same source.

Klaus explained that he had been given his watch by one of the United Arab Republic rulers, and Wilma said so had she. Klaus explained that five or six years previously he was phoned by the Austrian Foreign Ministry saying he must drop everything and fly at once to the UAE where one of the rulers, who was a good friend of Austria, had skin problems. Klaus flew out from Vienna the same day and arrived in Dubai late at night. He was met by a Polish pilot who appeared a little intoxicated. The pilot explained that the sheik was hunting in the desert and that he would fly Klaus out in a little single engined aircraft that very night. It is not an exaggeration to say that Klaus was more than very concerned about his chances of survival on the flight which turned out to be very bumpy. Eventually the plane landed, and Klaus was led to a tent which had all the necessary facilities. Klaus was even more upset when the sheik kept him waiting in the tent for three days. His minions explained that he was out hunting, and this was clearly more important than dermatological matters. Eventually Klaus was ushered into the ruler's tent and the skin problem was clear. The sheik was infested by mites which on balance emanated from his hunting birds. Klaus explained what the problem was and what steps were necessary to rectify it. He was given a gold Rolex watch and $1,000 US dollars for his troubles and was flown back to Dubai by the Polish pilot who, on this occasion, appeared to be sober and then flew back to Vienna on a scheduled airline. The whole process had taken the best part of a week.

Klaus said he was summoned out on three or four more occasions to see this sheik. The problem was always the same and he was sure his life would end in a plane crash in the desert if this problem continued. Therefore, when asked to drop everything and go out to the UAE again just before Christmas, one year he declined.

It was then that Wilma was contacted in the States and was asked to go immediately to the UAE by the US State Department who said that the Emirate was a very close ally of the USA and US-UAE relations were at stake. Wilma was Jewish but she was not going to drop everything just prior to enjoying Christmas. She asked the State Department to tell the ruler that Christmas was a christian festival and that she would go out in the New Year, which she did. She was met at the airport in Dubai and taken to the Emirate concerned. On this occasion the Emir was at home in his palace and Wilma was driven there and housed in the hareem with more than several wives and concubines. She was kept waiting in the hareem for three or four days and eventually she was ushered into Emir's presence. He proved very reluctant to show his 'best bits' to a woman. The problem was a mite infestation from his hunting birds – just as Klaus had found. Wilma however, solved the problem brilliantly. She prescribed an anti-mite cream and asked the ladies in the hareem to use this cream as a massage cream during the Emir's often and regular visits. She was given a gold Rolex and $1000 US dollars for her troubles which she decided not to declare to the US customs reasoning, quite rightly I think, that she had been on government business.

I was asked on one occasion to drop everything and fly out to the Middle East to see someone of importance, but I think wisely, I declined to go.

STREPTOMYCIN

Streptomycin was an antibiotic discovered in the USA a little time after penicillin. It revolutionised the treatment of tuberculosis, until then, a massive world killer, but it had its drawbacks in that it was not absorbed by mouth and had to be given by injection. It is totally ineffective orally.

Mrs Q was a married woman in her fifties but looked a lot older. She had suffered for many years from systemic lupus erythematosus (SLE) a potentially fatal and multi-system auto-immune disease where the body attacks itself and in normally treated by oral steroids.

Mrs Q was admitted with a fever and investigations showed she had a septicaemia together with infection around her heart in her pericardial sac. Blood cultures were carried out and I also aspirated the pericardial sac with great anxiety and both the blood culture and culture of the pus from the pericardial sac grew the same organism which was sensitive to streptomycin. I asked our houseman (a lady recently qualified) to put the patient on streptomycin. However, despite this medication Mrs Q continued to deteriorate and became gravely ill. I discussed her management with the bacteriologist who suggested we treat Mrs Q with gentamicin, a newly discovered antibiotic, as she had failed to respond to streptomycin. In those very early days, we were not sure how to administer gentamicin, but the drug saved her life. Sadly she was left permanently deaf, one of the now recognised problems with this particular antibiotic. When I told the pharmacy about the change in antibiotics the young pharmacist said "Thank God, we have had an awful time trying to make up streptomycin for oral use"! Our housewoman had prescribed the streptomycin orally. I could not imagine a graduate of any UK medical school being able to qualify not knowing that streptomycin must always be given by injection.

Postscript:

Mrs Q was not a patient of mine but a patient of one of my senior colleagues. In medicine it is best not to assume anything. Doubt and uncertainty should accompany you at all times, particularly at the bedside. Later I learnt that the lady houseman concerned did not continue in clinical medicine but chose public health instead. Possibly a wise decision. Somehow, however, we had failed her as medical teachers.

Tuberculosis continues to be a huge problem around the world commonly associated with HIV infection. Drug resistant tuberculosis is a common problem particularly where antimicrobial drug administration has been intermittent. This problem has been solved to some extent by medical surveillance techniques and more recently by the use of information technology to ensure that the drugs have been given and or taken.

Professor Selman Waxman received a medical Nobel Prize in 1952 for discovering streptomycin. In reality he had nothing to do with it and it was one of his researchers in his laboratory, Albert Schatz, who did all the work; this was not recognised until many years later. Waxman became rich and famous, Schatz was shafted. Waxman bullied his junior researcher into signing away all the rights to his discovery while secretly cutting a deal worth millions of dollars with the pharmaceutical company Merck.

VIRGIN BIRTH

Practising medicine is a great privilege and during a long career you can expect to come across some unusual events. For instance, I have read that each year more than seven hundred women of childbearing age in the States allege they have had a virgin birth. However, an apparently real virgin birth was recorded in the South African medical press some years ago.

The young black woman who was admitted in labour denied any previous sexual intercourse, and indeed, her hymen was intact which strongly supported her contention. The doctors involved noticed a large scar on her upper abdomen and asked the patient about it. The story was intriguing.

The young woman said she had a regular boyfriend and that about nine months previously she was having oral sex with another man who ejaculated into her mouth. A few seconds later the regular boyfriend arrived and not unexpectedly took exception to the situation. The man fled leaving the woman to face the consequences and her regular boyfriend was so angry he stabbed her in her upper abdomen and the wound was deep enough to penetrate the stomach wall. Emergency surgery was carried out to repair the stomach and abdominal wall successfully.

How did she get pregnant? It was thought the woman must either have swallowed the semen which had then escaped through the lacerated stomach into the peritoneal cavity or that some of the semen was present on the abdominal wall and entered the abdominal cavity with the knife. However, on balance the sperm continued their travels until one sperm fertilised an egg. This involved a long swim for the sperm involved.

Postscript:

You have to have some luck in life, but the South African woman had very little. On the other hand, her healthy baby had all the luck in the world.

nuts

As a NHS consultant I was obliged to undertake domiciliary visits (DV's) – home visits at the request of a patient's GP. Such visits were necessary for instance when the patient was too ill to travel to the hospital or when there was some urgency or doubt about the diagnosis. When I became a consultant dermatologist in 1973, you were obliged to do 50 DV's before you were paid so there was no incentive to do any. The whole situation changed radically two or three years later when our employer, the Yorkshire Regional Hospital Board, agreed to pay for all DV's up to a total of three hundred per year. This led to quite a lot of abuse of the system both by GPs and consultants. GPs would ask for a DV to short circuit an out-patient appointment and get their patients seen quickly. Some consultants saw this as a way of augmenting their income as a standard fee plus mileage was paid and the fee was pensionable.

One consultant radiologist in Grimsby was rumoured to do domiciliary visits, but he had no portable x-ray equipment, and a senior colleague was deputed to go and see him and warn him about his fraud. It was also alleged that a consultant from the Indian continent in a West Riding town and his GP cousin, worked the system, chalking up three hundred domiciliary visits and sharing the proceeds. There was also a story that one consultant had his secretary draw a large graph on his office wall to record every DV and when a total of three hundred was reached, she had to decline any future GP requests which were then referred to colleagues. The problem was that this particular consultant usually managed to do his yearly total of three hundred visits in just three months and it meant that his two colleagues were busier than usual after that. Some General

Practitioners liked the system and used the DV avidly and wanted to continue with it even after the three hundred maximum had been reached. In theory the GPs were supposed to accompany the consultant but rarely did. If a GP wanted to accompany me, I would try and get to the house five or ten minutes earlier so I could take my own history rather than have a GP struggle with a fat Lloyd George Medical Record folder. There were many apocryphal tales about DVs – the surgeon asked to do a DV on a man with possible rectal carcinoma. Apparently, he managed to do a rectal examination on the patient's twin brother. There was also a tale about a gynaecologist who arrived at the house with no gloves in his bag, but despite this the gynaecologist managed to examine the patient in question. There is also the gynaecologist who managed to examine a woman living next door to the real patient.

Some estates in Leeds were rough; Gipton in particular was a prime example. You had to drive carefully to avoid bricks and other debris in the road and if you were wise, you would arrange for your car aerial to be retracted as this was a ready target for local youths. Dogs were an ever-present threat. In Gipton dogs were turfed out of their homes, often hungry, in the morning and formed wolf-packs not averse to attacking strangers. One of my colleagues had his suit removed by such a pack and was only rescued because a council worker emerged from a hole in the road with a metal rod and beat the dogs off. After a lot of pleadings, the Regional Hospital Board reimbursed my colleague for a new suit.

This colleague – Bill was asked to see a lady in a poor part of Leeds because she had a non-healing leg ulcer. Bill carried out a DV rather late in the evening after a long day at work in the hospital. He knocked at the door and went straight into the lounge/dining room and found himself facing a dog which looked reasonably friendly. Bill introduced himself as he walked across the black filthy carpet which was sticking to his shoes. The woman's dressing had slipped around her ankles and the dog gave the infected leg ulcer a lick from time to time.

"Would you like a nice cup of tea?" the patient asked. Bill replied quickly "No thanks I have just had one." It is almost axiomatic that women with black sticky carpets almost always offer you a nice cup of tea. Bill examined the patient helped by the licking dog and left a note for the district nurse about future management. Just as he was going out the patient asked Bill if he would like some nuts to eat on his way home as he must be hungry and because it was fairly late. Bill felt tempted but the woman was evidently poor so he declined and said she should keep the nuts and enjoy them herself; he would come back and assess her leg ulcer in a month.

One month later Bill returned. The ulcer was improving, his DV was again in the late evening and once more he was offered nuts to eat on his way home. He was rather hungry so after some protestation he took the nuts and assuaged his hunger whilst driving home. They tasted quite good. Bill reviewed the patient for the last time six weeks later, again late in the evening. By now the ulcer was healing well and once more he was offered some nuts for his home journey. Bill protested again but the patient insisted saying that her daughter brought her some chocolates every week so she licked off the chocolate coating and kept the nuts, which she did not like, for Bill. I gather he vomited on his way out of the house.

ETHEL

As medical students we were given a clinical lecture once a week by one of the medical or university staff at the Royal Victoria Infirmary in Newcastle. Some of these lectures were more memorable than others and this is an account of one of the most memorable.

Ethel was brought into the lecture theatre which was full with one hundred and fifty to two hundred clinical students by professor Martin Roth, the then professor of psychiatry in Newcastle. Ethel in her twenties was not beautiful. She was rotund, dumpy and fat with rather poor-quality hair and red telangiectatic cheeks. She looked extremely alarmed and anxious when she saw the size of the audience.

Professor Roth said rather abruptly that Ethel's problem was that she stammered and had done so all her life, "Isn't that right?" Ethel could only stutter and nod. No recognisable sound came out of her mouth. Professor Roth continued to interrogate Ethel in a rather aggressive way. "Isn't it true you were left-handed and were made to be right-handed?" he demanded, and Ethel did her best to reply but could only stutter and nod her head. Roth explained that it was quite common for people with a stammer to have been forced to change handedness as a child. He continued to interrogate Ethel aggressively and we as students were getting uneasy at his tactics of history taking. Ethel began to cry. Surely Roth had gone too far.

Roth turned to Ethel and said, "A lot of people with a stammer join a choir because they can sing without stammering, are you in a choir?" Ethel tearfully indicated she was. We medical students were very hostile and restless now and ready to have a verbal go at Roth. How could he be so intimidating and lack any compassion? "Are you in a church choir?" he demanded. She stuttered and nodded but no sound came out. "Will you sing with me?" he demanded; Ethel stuttered assent. By now the student audience were more than hostile. Professor Roth, who was Jewish, asked if they could sing Onward Christian Soldiers together. Ethel agreed but was still unable to speak.

Roth began singing and Ethel joined in, her tears gone and with a beautiful voice sang verse after verse of the hymn perfectly.

They finished together to thunderous applause from the students. In the space of a few minutes Roth had not only turned his audience from being incredibly hostile to being amazed, but he had also done far more for Ethel therapeutically. She was smiling and her self-esteem was obviously increased massively.

Professor Roth went on to become professor of psychiatry at Oxford and then President of the Royal College of Psychiatrists. He was Knighted for his contribution to psychiatry.

Professor Roth was a great communicator and seemed to be able to quote at length for example effortlessly from English literature. A friend of mine spent some time training in his department. He told me Roth was extremely nervous before any lecture and would even spend some time on the toilet before his presentation. During my life as a medical practitioner I had the opportunity of talking to performers such as actors and pianists who often asserted they do not perform on their top form unless they are a little nervous before a performance. The trick is not to get over-anxious or go the other way and give a very complacent lecture.

Some years later when I was working as a medical registrar, I admitted a man thought to have had a coronary, but he could not talk only stammer, so I asked him to sing his replies to my questions which he did but it was two thirty am in the male ward and the other patients were not too happy about this solution.

THE DANGERS OF MEDICINE

Medicine can be a dangerous business. Doctors and nurses have been killed by pandemics and it is known for instance that doctors having done a long night shift are more likely to be involved in a road traffic accident driving home. I have been attacked by a patient on at least two occasions: first was a man with a large flowerpot which he wanted to smash over my head in casualty and secondly later as a registrar in training by a patient who became manic as a result of his treatment with corticosteroids. Could corticosteroids be responsible for President Trump's manic behaviour during and after his recent inpatient stay with Covid 19. Treatment with dexamethasone, a potent corticosteroid, is now routine.

Doctors have been murdered by patients. For example, two plastic surgeons were murdered by a psychiatric Iraqi patient in Wakefield. At least one psychiatrist has been murdered in Leeds. Doctors working in war zones are particularly vulnerable. Suicide is a feature of medical practice and psychiatrists, and anaesthetists are more likely to seek this exit from life than doctors in other specialities. Happily, suicide in dermatology is very rare.

You would think that dermatology as a speciality would be immune from danger. Not so. One problem is that some emollients contain liquid paraffin and are easily set on fire. One patient in Doncaster is alleged to have died as a result of burns linked to this chemical. Some hand liquids designed to sterilise the skin contain alcohol and burns have occurred in patients lighting a cigarette after using alcohol hand preparations. One of my housemen and his patient got a nasty shock. The patient had large warts in the genital area which were to be cauterised under local anaesthetic. The young doctor prepped the area with an antiseptic and injected a local anaesthetic. The first wart was treated with a hot glowing cautery. In an instant, the patient caught fire, mercifully only transiently as the skin prep contained alcohol. The fire was sufficient to deprive the patient of her pubic hair but was not severe enough to merit the use of a fire extinguisher or produce any skin burns.

ESTHER

I first met Esther and her much older husband Maurice in my Harrogate private consulting rooms. Maurice (his adopted UK name) was Jewish and had fled the Nazi terror from Vienna in the nineteen thirties, spending much of the war interned in the Isle of Man. He subsequently went on to run a very successful engineering business and was so immersed in this that he did not get around to looking for a wife until he was quite elderly. He met Esther who was a young widow at the time at the local synagogue when Esther was in her thirties. The business was sold when Maurice reached the age of sixty for several million pounds. Esther took the care of Maurice under her wing. At the least appearance or suggestion of a medical problem Maurice was taken to see the GP.

On the day I first met the couple, they arrived during a severe thunderstorm and Maurice and his wife were drenched despite umbrellas. Most of my patients had phoned to re-book their consultations because of the severe weather but not Esther. The medical problem was trivial, an ingrowing toenail. I explained the only way of dealing with this was to do a wedge excision of the nail in continuity with the nail bed which could be done easily under a local anaesthetic. Esher, however, was very concerned Maurice would find this procedure too uncomfortable and asked if I could do the surgery under a general anaesthetic. I was not too enthusiastic as Maurice was approaching eighty years of age and was receiving a large range of medication for high blood pressure and angina. However, Esther persisted, and Maurice seemed to go along with it passively.

I remained concerned so I rang Maurice's GP who explained his greatest problem was Esther - how to keep her away from taking Maurice to doctors and hospital. Esther had recently moved house to live next door to their GP so any of Maurice's medical problems could be dealt with as quickly as possible. By now Maurice had had a series of minor operations but all under general anaesthetic. The GP was faced with a conflict. Was Esther genuinely concerned about her husband or trying to kill him with kindness? We shall never know. Maurice died shortly afterwards ater a prostatectomy but Esther had found she could persuade almost any surgeon to operate as she and her husband were private patients.

Postscript:

Esther now widowed for the second time developed a relationship with the family chauffer and bought several racehorses. Would the chauffer have to watch his back and how did her first husband die? Was this killing by kindness or was she generally devoted to Maurice? We shall never know.

It is interesting that some years ago there was a doctor's strike in Israel during which the death rate fell significantly!

A NORWEIGIAN SAGA

In 1981 I was asked to give a series of lectures in Norway. I arranged to take my 17 year-old daughter with me together with my elderly parents who loved Norway. Sadly, two months previously my mother had to have a total gastrectomy for stomach cancer, and she was still quite frail. Together we flew from Leeds\Bradford Airport courtesy of Brown Air in a seven-seater twin engined plane. I will always remember the look of acute alarm on my mother's face as we took off. She had never travelled in such a small plane before. The flight had been over-booked, and one passenger was sitting on some luggage at the back of the aircraft. I acted as an air hostess serving the drinks which most of the passengers needed to steady their nerves. Despite some anxiety we all arrived safely in Oslo and spent about ten days in Norway.

We were the first to check in for the return journey and we were told that the Brown Air flight was over-booked. On this occasion there were fourteen passengers and only ten seats, so four passengers were asked to volunteer to fly back to London Heathrow on a British Airways flight. One of those volunteering was my daughter and another a young Norwegian student returning to Leeds University to re-sit his finals the following morning. My parents were elderly, and my mother was very frail, so we three were allowed to fly back to Leeds. The co-pilot had been kicked off the flight and I was accommodated in his seat alongside the pilot. The reader would be interested to know that sometime after this Brown Air went bankrupt after they tried to institute regular flights between Leeds/Bradford and Luton as a quick way to get to London.

The day had also been eventful for British Airways. A Boeing 737 developed severe engine problems during take-off from Manchester Airport and as a result the whole of the British Airways fleet of Boeing 737's had been grounded. Consequently, British Airways put an old Tri-Star into service and this aircraft was to pick up passengers from Stockholm, Copenhagen and also Oslo for Heathrow.

When this old plane tried to land at Heathrow the undercarriage failed to operate so the plane circled around to use up some fuel and the passengers were prepared for a crash landing. On the final approach, which was very tense, the pilot managed to get the undercarriage down but the stress for all the passengers was enormous. The plane landed very late at night, but my daughter managed to get to Kings Cross and was allowed to sit on a stack of newspapers on the newspaper train from London to York and I picked her up from York station at about three in the morning. On the way back to Leeds we were nearly wiped out by a fox straying onto the road. After such an eventful day I wondered if the Norwegian student had managed to get to Leeds for his vital re-sit.

I was exceptionally busy on returning to work, but I began to reflect on the Norwegian student's difficulties and the stress he must have been under. At this time, I was an honorary senior lecturer in dermatology at Leeds University, so I decided to ring the University Registrar telling him how the student had been bumped off his flight from Oslo and moreover had to go through the experience of expecting a crash landing at Heathrow, not to mention the potential problems of getting to Leeds in time for his resit. Because of all these difficulties I had to conclude that this student, on balance, had little or no sleep the previous night.

The Registrar thanked me for the information and rang me back the following day telling me that the Norwegian student had failed, albeit narrowly. However, he had not mentioned any of his difficulties to his tutor which I thought was amazing.

Armed with the new information I had provided, his paper was reviewed, and he was awarded a pass and his degree. I had to agree never to divulge the Norwegian's name and I readily agreed because I never knew it.

Postscript:

You need a bit of good luck in life and in this case considerable initial bad luck led ultimately to good fortune. I hope this young man went on to have a long and successful career. I shall never know.

OSBORNE

I grew up in Sheffield and like all children I was obliged to take the eleven plus exam. The exam was in two parts, and I received no special training at my primary school. Moreover, I was not expected to pass. The problem was that the result of this exam at such an early stage in your life would determine many aspects of your future life. Pass and the opportunities were almost limitless. Fail and you would probably be faced with the reality of a working life of drudgery with poor financial prospects.

We lived in a district of Sheffield called Wadsley, not far from the later to become the notorious Hillsborough football ground, home to Sheffield Wednesday. Opposite our home on the other side of the road lived the Hattersley family and son Roy. Mrs Hattersley was a member of the Co-operative movement and later became a socialist mayor of Sheffield. Roy was sent to a private primary school called Oakdale and in due course passed his eleven plus for the City Grammar School. Roy (later Lord Hattersley) was one of the first students to read economics at the new university of Hull and graduated with a first-class honours degree. No doubt this held him in good stead later when he became a socialist Chancellor of the Exchequer. Roy's success illustrates neatly the potential importance of the eleven plus exam.

I can remember taking the second part of the exam on a snowy morning in Wadsley Church School, and lobbing a snowball through the door into the classroom after the exam was over. In retrospect, I think this action was an expression of my anger at the exam and the almost certainty I would fail. To my surprise a letter arrived home some weeks later saying that I had passed and had been selected to go to High Storrs

Grammar School on the south side of Sheffield a good hour's journey from my home by tram with a long walk at both ends of the journey.

I arrived at my new school in September 1951 wearing a smart school uniform which, was in itself, a new experience after primary school. I was sitting next to Osborne. I never knew his Christian name, but he wore a blazer which was too small for him and a cap which was too large. He had a very broad Sheffield accent, and his face was pale with fine wrinkles. He looked undernourished in his uniform which was obviously second hand. At primary school we all called each other by our Christian names but at the Grammar School we called each other by our family names.

The English master by way of introduction asked us all to write about our first impressions of the new school in an essay as homework. The 29 members of the class including myself wrote some rubbish aimed at pleasing the English master, but Osborne wrote something very different.

In his essay Osborne included the fact that we were all called by our surname and not by our first names. Furthermore, Osborne in his perceptive essay observed that each teacher in his new school had a nickname which Osborne proceeded to list. The list of names included "Chad, Black Death, Conk, Billy Bags" and many more. It was almost complete and very accurate. It was not an understatement to say that the English master was unimpressed by Osborne's originality. He threw Osborne's essay on the floor and appeared to have some difficulty speaking but managed to enquire "Are you mad boy?" After a long verbal dressing down Osborne was given a detention for his audacity. In a flash all Osborne's creativity had been extinguished and no doubt he went on to face a life of conformity like most of the class.

Postscript:

Grammar schools enable some pupils to thrive and go on to great things, but sadly there were some students like Osborne who did not conform to the system and were destined mainly therefore, to fail. Our teachers have an enormous responsibility to make sure creativity flourishes. Sadly, I don't know where Osborne is now and how his life panned out. I hope his psyche survived this brutal attack. Some go on to great things despite their teachers.

The eleven plus examination system was terminated in most parts of England and replaced by the comprehensive school. Suzie, my eldest daughter, was one of the first pupils to receive a comprehensive school education. When she reached the age of 16 my wife and I were invited to her school by the headmistress who told us that she saw no good prospects for Suzie and that she should leave school without taking any O levels and try and get a job in a shoe shop. I protested and told the headmistress I thought my daughter was as bright as any other medical students I had taught. In the event, I had to pay for my daughter to take the O levels so certain was the headmistress that she would fail. My daughter lived on her wits, did a fortnights work and passed all ten O levels with good grades. After obtaining a good law degree at university she was called to the bar and has had a very successful career as a barrister, and still living on her wits.

SEAN

Sean and his brother grew up in a tiny back-to-back in the poorest part of Sunderland. The toilet was outside, newspapers served as toilet paper and a bath was possible once a week in a zinc tub in front of the fire. Sean developed tuberculosis necessitating 2 years in a sanatorium. Sean had passed his 'A' levels and was admitted to medical school subsequently. He was bright enough to win a bursary to study physiology for a further year leading to an Honours BSc degree. Only three or four students would be selected to read physiology each year at this stage of their student career. During the year out reading physiology, Sean had to complete a project and write his findings to satisfy part of the degree requirements. Sean developed a dip stick to test for sugar in urine. Unfortunately, he told his tutor to "fuck off" during the course and as a result was awarded a third-class Honours degree, which in reality is a fail.

Postscript:

Had Sean patented his idea, he would have become very rich. Dip sticks to measure sugar in the urine are now used routinely all over the world but Sean was first in the field. The problem was like Osborne, he refused to conform.

On the other hand Sean was a devout Catholic and had a regular girlfriend at university. He was terribly conflicted and because of his faith there were no sexual relations between the two of them for the six years he was at medical school. In this regard Sean conformed entirely with the teachings of the Roman Catholic church.

Sean was very creative and constructed some Northumbrian pipes during his houseman year and he was able to play these exceptionally well.

After qualifying Sean married another young woman, the daughter of a pathologist. Sadly, the marriage did not work, and Sean began to train as a psychiatrist. He told me one morning he totally "lost it" when a very neurotic woman came in complaining of almost everything. Sean lost his cool and told her she was bloody lucky that she had not experienced all the problems he'd had in life. On reflection Sean decided he did not have any future in psychiatry and took up radiology. He became a well-liked and good radiologist in Leicester. Sadly, he developed colon cancer at a young age, but was attending German night classes up to a fortnight before his death. Sean liked his alcohol and in the last days of his life was in a hospice in Leicester. Because of his religion he declined any strong opiate medication, so I took a bottle of good malt whisky down when I went to see him, and we shared the contents of the bottle and some of our life experiences.

A SCOTTISH SURGEON

George grew up in Glasgow in a tenement block in the Gorbals. Like many teenagers he joined a gang and told me he had nearly killed members of opposing gangs. George was very bright and was never apprehended by the police, whilst other gang members were less fortunate and ended up in jail. George told me one became totally broken after a birching whilst another learnt to play football whilst in borstal and ended up playing for that famous Scottish football team Rangers. George explained there was considerable friction between the supporters of Celtic and Rangers. Celtic was largely supported by the Roman Catholic community whilst Rangers was supported by the Protestant community. During a match wounded fighting spectators would be brought to casualty from both camps and George said it was usual for hostilities to resume in casualty where it was prudent to wait until the warring sides had exhausted themselves before attending to their wounds.

The Scottish education system enabled gifted youngsters from the poorest backgrounds to progress to university and this was a path taken by George who was admitted to medical school in the nineteen fifties. After qualification in Glasgow, George trained as a surgeon and undertook National Service as a Medical Officer in the Black Watch, a famous Scottish Regiment, with a final rank of major and based in Stirling Castle.

Prior to this army service George had worked briefly as a GP in the Gorbals when he was called out one evening to see a man on the top floor of a tenement building. George said he was breathless when he knocked on the door and entered the apartment and was confronted by a woman who looked to be in her sixties and said, 'He's in there,' indicating a bedroom door. George entered the bedroom and found an elderly man who was obviously dead and so obvious was this to him that he did not carry out a thorough examination to confirm death irrefutably. George was a man of very few words and an absent bedside manner. "He's dead," he said to the woman whom he presumed was the man's wife and walked out. Halfway down the almost endless stairs of the tenement the woman shouted down to him. "He's done it before." Christ, thought George, I will have to go back. He retraced his steps and this time he examined the man thoroughly. The man was indeed dead and if as alleged he had done it successfully before he had certainly failed on this last occasion.

George was eventually appointed a general surgeon in Harrogate and was trained as a vascular surgeon, capable of repairing aortic aneurisms. George was a born surgeon, gifted with great surgical dexterity coupled with a passionate desire to always do the very best for each of his individual patients which often got him into conflict with hospital managers.

George became in great demand because his only two surgical consultant colleagues were somewhat problematical. One would only operate on a narrow range of potentially 'safe' surgical challenges whilst the other colleague had earlier been involved in a severe road traffic accident resulting in frontal lobe brain damage and rendering him disinhibited. This colleague could only take on relatively minor surgical problems and if he got into surgical difficulties, George was called to bail him out.

George liked to have a beer on his way home in an attractive pub on the side of the River Nidd popular with locals and tourists alike until the pub became invaded by a group of Hell's Angels. This led to most of the locals and even tourists deserting the pub. The bikers were very disruptive breaking pub furnishings and fittings and foul mouthing any remaining customers. The publican called the police repeatedly, but they declined to be of any assistance. The landlord was desperate and faced with ruin.

George explained to the landlord that he may be able to help as an ex-member of the Black Watch he could contact the Regiment at any time if he was experiencing 'difficulties' and the regiment would usually help. The Hell's Angels were disrupting George's quality of life, so it was increasingly difficult for him to relax over a beer in the pub. George told me in his view this was ample justification to ask for the Regiment's help. As a result of George's request, two members of the Black Watch were despatched; neither wore uniform and the two sat quietly in the pub as the bikers arrived. Almost immediately the Hell's Angels began to abuse George and the two soldiers in mufti who were trained fighters and enjoyed their job. George told me within a twinkle of an eye, these two trained killers got to work on the astonished and totally unprepared bikers who were about 20 in number. Bodies flew out of the door and even one went through the windows leaving a heap of bleeding humanity on the pavement outside the pub. The Scottish warriors walked outside and stood over their victims telling them "If any of you fuckers come back, we will fucking kill you!" It was not surprising there were no more problems in the pub.

George told me this story after I mentioned my daughter was having death threats whilst studying at Essex University. As a result, George offered me a regimental solution which I declined. This was a worrying time both for me and my daughter and the left-wing Vice Chancellor seemed less than interested. The culprit was eventually found and turned out to be a woman of colour unmarried with child. The police were not involved when the university fined the woman £600 which was apparently raised during a Lesbian/Gay get together.

Postscript:

Sometimes it becomes necessary to meet force with force. Currently the Police forces in the UK are under severe pressure because of austerity cuts and ever burgeoning bureaucracy. Gangland culture involving knives has become commonplace especially in London.

The drug laws fail to help, and prohibition has never worked. Decriminalisation of drugs would go a very long way towards diminishing the power, criminality, and influence of drug gangs. Prohibition has cost billions of pounds and dollars and merely ensures the drug barons become more and more wealthy whilst being rarely apprehended. Almost all medical opinion in the UK favours de-criminalisation but the politicians so far have failed to act. As I write this book the government has announced a 10-year programme to crack down on the drug culture in this country. Sadly, it is destined to fail. Decriminalisation of drug usage in Portugal has led to a significant reduction not only in drug use but also in drug associated crime.

A VERY GOOD DEATH

My wife and I had a twenty-year-old white cat who managed us very well and we were very fond of him. He was called 'white boy.' Sadly, he began to pass blood in his urine, so I was deputed to take him to the vet one evening. The vet examined the cat very carefully and found a tumour on one of his kidneys. There was no option in view of his age but to euthanise him. I rang my wife asking her if she would like to see the cat for the last time before this procedure, but she declined tearfully. The vet gave the cat a sedative by injection into his neck which did not seem to cause any feline distress and the cat continued to purr as I stroked him on the examination table. Thirty minutes later the vet returned and examined the cat and concluded he was sedated enough for the administration of a lethal injection. The cat appeared to suffer no distress during this injection and continued purring to within five seconds of his death, as I continued to stroke him.

Postscript:

Why can't we treat human beings like this? It is known that the majority of adults in the UK (about 75%) favour assisted death when the time is right, but politicians continue to fail to reflect the views of their constituents. However, currently I gather there are political moves afoot to legalise human self-assisted death or even euthanasia.

A VERY BAD DEATH

Years before we had another white cat, a male, who was also very old and also called 'white boy'. One sunny Sunday afternoon he had a stroke. We rang the vet, a Scotsman of few words who was obviously not best pleased to be disturbed on a sunny Sunday afternoon He barked at me down the phone in a heavy Glaswegian accent to bring the cat to the surgery. I rang the bell, and the little Glaswegian vet opened the door in silence. We placed the cat gently on the vet's table. Meanwhile the vet who said nothing appeared to be drawing up some fluid into a syringe with a large needle. Without a word he plunged the needle into the cat with such force it was propelled across the table and would have fallen off the table but for my wife's position. "You have killed my cat" my wife shouted at the vet. "What did ye expect?" he replied - the first words he had spoken to us. In his second attempt at conversation, he asked for his fee. I paid the man. Both my wife and I were very distressed that we had been a party to such an ill-treatment of our cat. We both felt we had let him down badly.

Postscript:

The treatment of this cat was in stark contrast of the treatment of our other cat. Why do people want to become vets if they treat animals like this? In a way, what happened to the second cat is a metaphor of the present human situation when people are near to death. A large 'needle' is symbolic of 'last medical human rights' consisting of intravenous drips, expensive antibiotics, steroids and oxygen. Why do we as a society and as doctors and nurses not strive to let people die peacefully? To prolong life is a noble aim but the quality of that prolonged life is vital. Continuing and medicalising the agony for me is not on. Too often the palliative care cohort of our profession seems too fearful about the possibility of lawyers looking over their shoulders. Moreover, as a society we can no longer afford to pay the enormous costs of final medical bills.

I have advanced prostatic cancer and I hope to die well and in control. I would hope to receive appropriate palliative care when the time is right. I would not expect to be deprived of fluids and food unless I wanted to be. I would not want any valiant attempts to 'save my life' and I would hope one of my daughters might hold my hand when the time comes to 'drop off the perch'.

It is a good policy to make an advanced medical directive and this can include funeral arrangements if you wish. I have requested that my family arrange my last journey to the crematorium, and I hope not to be late for this appointment. I have also requested that besides some Mozart the song 'return to sender, address unknown' is also played. I have asked for my ashes to be scattered around the tenth tee at Headingley Golf Club if I die in England and around the ninth green at Castro Marim Golfe Club should I die in Portugal. Should I manage to drop off the perch in New Zealand I have asked for my ashes to be scattered around the fifth green of Queenstown Golf Club. Should I die in Italy, I have asked for my ashes to be scattered on my little truffle farm there.

SOME MORE REFLECTIONS ON DEATH

I am writing these reflections in my eighty first year. Years ago, in the nineteen sixties I worked as a junior doctor on a medical firm in Ipswich. The charge nurse (Willie) was in control of the nursing on the male ward and was referred to in whispers by his peers as 'the little reaper'. Willie operated a small two bedded unit just off the corridor which led to the main ward. Men with profound medical problems such as a severe stroke which had led to unconsciousness would be nursed in this small unit. Willie would make sure that all the windows were left open even during the winter and it was accepted that patients never got out of this side ward alive. A terminal pneumonia was often the best friend an old man could have.

Forty years later when this hospital had been demolished and Willie himself was long since dead, one of the junior doctors who worked with me at the time told me Willie would help his 'no hope' patients on their way using insulin. I was horrified by this information but the doctor who gave me this information is now also dead. My informant Dr Ann had an interesting career following her time with me in Ipswich. She became resident paediatrician to the Sultan of Brunei's children. This work was not too exacting and entailed a lot of first-class air travel around the world. Later when the Sultan's children had grown up, Dr Ann worked as a GP in a very deprived area of London not far from Kings College Hospital. She never married and had a passion for Dalmatians and gin. Usually two of her dogs would accompany her during a home visit. She took on Dalmatians with behavioural problems from a society which was dedicated to Dalmatian dog rescue.

One night she was attacked by men of colour who had called her out with the sole intention of robbing her and stealing any drugs she might have with her in the car. Dr Ann sustained a severe head injury and the two dogs with her were killed. The head injury left her with significant neurological problems forcing her to retire to a small cottage in the countryside in Kent. The cottage was very isolated and Dr Ann adopted two more Dalmatians to share the cottage with her. Sadly, sometime later her brother found her dead in the cottage and a Coroner's post-mortem found she had had a heart attack. She had been dead for a number of days before her brother found her and by this time, stimulated by hunger, her dogs began to eat her so that she was unrecognisable. What a tragic end.

It is an unwritten law in many communities around the world that the doctor is never attacked by criminal gangs. This is because the doctor may be necessary to attend to an injured member of a gang at any time in the future. This code no longer exists in this country and sadly in many areas, it can be darn right dangerous to undertake home visits in day time let alone at night – a commentary on the society we now live in.

Postscript:

Recently a German nurse has been convicted of killing over a hundred patients and Beverly Allit (a nurse) used insulin during her killing spree in the UK. Harold Shipman a well-liked single-handed GP probably killed over two hundred and fifty of his patients, mostly elderly using opioids. In the early nineteen sixties Dr Bodkin Adams, an Eastbourne GP, was accused of murdering some of his rich elderly female patients for financial gain but was found 'not guilty'. Recently perhaps over four hundred patients have had their lives terminated prematurely in a cottage hospital in Gosport where the medical practitioner concerned still awaits justice.

Whilst almost all doctors follow the tenets of the Hippocratic Oath of 'first do no harm', it is noteworthy that most medial schools do not now require graduates to take the Hippocratic Oath or any of its modern equivalents. I feel we need a debate about end-of-life care urgently.

In particular is the act of assisting dying a help or a harm for the individual patient? This is clearly an area of conflict for politicians and the religious, but I feel the time has come to grasp the nettle and legislate democratically according to the majority view of the UK adult population. It is my view that an individual's body belongs to that individual who should have the ultimate say about what happens to it.

To meander away from death for a moment and return to the Sultan of Brunei and his family one of my best friends was a New Zeeland dermatologist, Peter Gould a very colourful character based in Auckland who looked after many celebrities including the Sultan of Brunei and his family.

Peter told me some years ago a daughter of the Sultan of Brunei rang him concerned about her acne and asked him to drop everything to go and see her at home. Peter explained that he was very busy and could she not fly to Auckland. She agreed. During the consultation Peter noted that she had just had her 21st birthday. "I bet your father gave you something spectacular for your birthday" he said. "He did" she replied " an Airbus I've come in it today"!

IRAN

The Dowling Club was founded in honour of Geoffrey Dowling, a distinguished dermatologist held in great awe by his peers. This is a Dermatological Travelling Club and now has almost 700 members scattered all around the world but mostly in the UK. The aim of the club is for seniors and young trainees to travel together from the UK to other dermatological centres in other parts of the world, both the young and the old learning from their hosts and each other as they go. I had the honour of being elected President of the Dowling Club in 1995 and took a group of young and older dermatologists to Mexico, San Francisco, Amsterdam, Utrecht and Marburg.

Years before I took part in a Dowling Club visit to Iran in the latter days of the Shah, shortly before the country became a theocracy. The country even then was in a certain amount of chaos. Our hotel in Tehran had been grossly overbooked and four of us had to share a single room on our first night in the capital. We saw plenty of road accidents and crossing the street was a work of art. Following our stay in Tehran we visited Shiraz where the Shah had a palace in the centre of a large military camp. We found some soldiers there actually cutting the grass with scissors. I left the group in Shiraz and travelled to Mashed, a very holy city in the Northeast of Iran near the Afghan border. I had been invited to give a lecture on tattoos in Mashed by professor Mostoufi who had spent two years in Leeds training in dermatology in my department. Tattoos in the then western style are forbidden by the Muslim faith and pictures of any sort on the skin are not allowed. You may acquire a tattoo if you were a Muslim, but it had to be for pragmatic reasons and only letters were allowed. An occasional tattoo could be seen in the Muslim world for example in people with migraine where a tattoo could appear on the forehead or temple or in an individual with arthritis overlying the affected joint. A similar Muslim culture forbids pictorial art in Mosques although there are occasional exceptions. In Damascus for example, when an ancient synagogue was incorporated into a more recent but still very old Mosque there was still some Judaic art present on the walls. On the flight into Mashed more attention was given to Muslim religious culture than on other air flights in Iran. The stewardesses wore burkas and alcoholic drinks were served but delivered to you on a tray covered by a black cloth.

I was staying with Professor Mostoufi and my lecture was two days hence. On the first day I had a wander around the old city. There was an ancient souk but as I got closer to the grand Mosque people began to spit at me, although the Shah had declared that infidels could visit any Mosque in Iran, but many Iranians particularly those in Mashed were not happy with this situation. I did some window shopping in the souk and identified some presents that I could buy for my daughters the following day after a bit of bartering.

When I went back to the souk the following day most of it had been bulldozed overnight to the ground. The souk had been in existence for centuries. It was horrendous. A crowd who I imagine were very angry store holders stood absolutely silent around the periphery of this vandalism. There were also many soldiers with machine guns ready for any trouble from the crowd. I was told later that the Shah's family wanted the site to build a supermarket. You can see why this regime was deposed. That night my host took me on a run to the Mosque in his car, but I had to exercise considerable caution keeping my head down.

Later I went for a drink in the Holiday Inn. My host had another appointment and I felt very isolated in this Muslim city. As I sipped my whisky, I caught sight of Dr Ronnie Scutt formerly Surgeon Captain Scuttt, dermatologist for the Royal Navy. Ronnie had recently retired from the Navy and was working for an international drug firm based in Beirut just before the civil war broke out in Lebanon. Ronnie had written a book on tattoos mainly based on his naval experiences and when the civil war came, he was appointed a consultant dermatologist in Lincolnshire. Ronnie and I had a good night. What a small world.

Ronnie was in the habit of taking his trousers down and showing his friends a large rose tattoo that he had on one thigh. He acquired this tattoo during a naval visit to Japan. Happily, on this occasion he kept his trousers on.

The following morning I went to the medical school lecture theatre with my slides and gave them to the projectionist, a rather obese middle-aged man who asked me if I liked Frank Sinatra. I replied "Yes' rather cautiously and he said he would play some of his music for me as the audience gathered. I was honoured by the attendance of the University Vice Chancellor, the Dean of the medical school and professors of many specialities including surgery, general medicine and dermatology. The lecture theatre was large, and I think held about three hundred people. It was full. The appointed time arrived for me to give my lecture, but nothing happened, Frank Sinatra continued to sing for another good half hour. The worthies in the front were looking a bit restless. Finally, the music stopped, and I was introduced. I gave my lecture and it seemed to go down well. The projectionist gave me back my slides, smiled and said he had enjoyed my talk. I said I had enjoyed Frank Sinatra and he smiled again.

I was told later that the projectionist was the most powerful man in the university and also in Mashed because his brother was a personal bodyguard and intimate of the Shah. That is why everyone had to wait until his music came to an end. He just enjoyed and loved hearing Frank Sinatra sing whatever the likes and dislikes of the audience.

THE DOCTOR FROM SRI LANKA

In our department we have trained several doctors from Sri Lanka over the years, and this was always a pleasure because graduates from the Medical School in Colombo were always very bright, efficient, good natured and dedicated doctors. Imagine my delight, therefore, when returning from my annual summer holidays I was told that we had a new Senior House Officer from Sri Lanka.

My first days back from holiday were very busy and I had a domiciliary request to see an elderly diabetic lady with a nasty infection on her leg (cellulitis) which was not responding to oral antibiotics. I went to see the patient as soon as possible. She needed urgent hospital treatment with intravenous fluids and antibiotics, and I suspected her diabetes would be out of control. I rang the newly appointed SHO. I was confident he would manage the situation well as his CV indicated he had done research into diabetes in Glasgow in the professorial medical unit before undertaking postgraduate studies leading to a PhD at Southampton university. Following that he had completed a year as a senior house officer in general medicine at Pinderfields Hospital in Wakefield just prior to joining our department.

I always liked to do my ward round on a one-to-one basis with a houseman or senior house officer and the ward sister. I did not like teaching hospital grand rounds with twenty or more health care workers around the patient's bed. This was very stressing for patients who were disadvantaged in any event by lying horizontal in their 'jim jams' on a Nightingale Ward with scant attention to privacy. Moreover, most of the grand round team, which included physiotherapists, pharmacists, social workers a ward sister and possibly staff nurses, 9 or 10 junior doctors of varying experience and 3 consultants contributed little or nothing to the patient's care, but anxiety. It was long drawn-out process which I always suspected was more to massage the ego of some of the more senior medical team than to be of benefit for the poor patients and offering a great opportunity for bullying particularly of the junior staff. The centre of attention should always be the patient. One study from Sweden showed that the grand round was an excellent facilitator of potentially fatal arrythmias in patients almost certainly due to the acute anxiety engendered by the process.

I remember seeing a man for medico-legal reasons. He had been admitted to a hospital in Yorkshire with a severe cellulitis in his leg and treated with intravenous antibiotics. During a grand round when the patient was feeling particularly vulnerable and wretched, a senior consultant alarmed his patient by drawing a line with a biro on the man's leg giving him no explanation. The patient immediately concluded, wrongly in the event, that this would be where his leg would be amputated. In reality the mark was put on the skin to indicate the extent of the cellulitis and any possible extension and would serve as a marker to indicate improvement or worsening.

The following morning, I met the doctor from Sri Lanka and told him that we would do a ward round together accompanied by the ward sister. Before the round I asked him about his aspirations. He said he wanted to get his membership so he could go home and become a consultant physician in Sri Lanka. The membership he wanted was of the Royal College of Physicians of London. This is not an easy exam to pass but I said I was very happy to help him and said that I would do a teaching round with him twice a week.

We came to the patient, the woman I had admitted the previous evening. To my surprise I found she was drowsy and very dehydrated. There was no intravenous drip for fluid or antibiotics, and I asked what her blood sugar was. The young doctor looked blank, and sister told me it was nearly 1000mg%

- enormously high. I asked how much insulin had she been given. Again, the doctor looked blank "none" said Sister.

The patient was in diabetic pre-coma. If we didn't act swiftly, she would go into coma and die. I asked the doctor how much insulin would he give? As a rule of thumb in those bad old days you divided the blood sugar level by ten indicating you would give one hundred units of insulin repeating the blood sugar two hours later and using the rule of ten again. I asked the doctor again how much insulin he would give the patient. To my amazement, after long cogitation he replied, "three units". I was almost speechless. Here was a doctor who had allegedly researched diabetes for a year giving me a totally ridiculous answer. I wrote the patient up for a hundred units of insulin and set up a drip to rehydrate her which contained the antibiotic she also needed. Happily, she recovered well.

I continued my ward round. The next patient had developed pernicious anaemia in the past a condition due to lack of vitamin B12, normally absorbed in the last part of the small intestine. I asked our new SHO where this vitamin was absorbed. After some thought he answered the colon. This is the large bowel and the answer he gave was totally absurd. I tried a bit of endocrinology asking him where testosterone, the male sex hormone, is synthesised. The right answer is the male testes. The Sri Lankan Doctor replied "the pituitary gland" a small gland at the base of the brain. I finished the round feeling very uneasy and went to see my senior colleague who had appointed this man. I related my serious concerns and said in my opinion his employment should be terminated as he was a potential danger to our patients. My colleague promised to talk to him but in the meantime, I asked the hospital HR department to photocopy the man's qualification data including his GMC registration. Rather worryingly I was told by the HR Department that they had only seen photocopies of his qualifications and no original documents. I sent the photocopies to the GMC (General Medical Council) with a letter voicing my concerns.

The following day my senior colleague asked to see me. He told me he had seen our new SHO and had found that he was very depressed. His father, a Sri Lankan GP, had almost died following a heart attack and his two children had been seriously ill. Moreover, he had not seen his family for over two years. His wife was very depressed about the whole situation. What a swine I felt. I was supposed to have a special interest in emotional, psychological and psychiatric aspects of dermatology and here I had failed to detect any of this young foreign doctor's anguish.

The next day was the grand round. It was noticeable that any probing questions about a patient or medicine was answered by one or more of the other junior staff, rather than the Sri Lankan doctor and his colleagues were clearly protecting him from any meaningful interrogation. To my mind this was yet another problem with the grand round. I looked at the treatment charts written up by our new young colleague. Every patient was prescribed the same basic drug regime which included an antibiotic, a diuretic (water tablet) and diazepam for night sedation - presumably designed to minimise any unwelcome night calls. Despite my senior colleague's lack of concern, I was very unhappy for now, but I let the matter drop.

About a week later I was doing my private rooms at home. The phone rang and my wife answered. She knocked on the consulting room door and white faced said the GMC were on the phone for me and wanted to talk to me urgently. I am sure my wife imagined I was about to be struck off!

The man from the GMC told me all the documents I had sent were forgeries and the police must be informed immediately. I was in the middle of seeing private patients, so my wife phoned my senior colleague, then doing a clinic in the LGI Outpatient Department. He refused to come to the phone when told that the GMC advice had been to call the police urgently and sent one of our senior registrars to take the call. I told him to call the police immediately and he said he would do so. Imagine my surprise when I went into work the following day to find the young Sri Lankan doctor in a white coat still working in the outpatient department.

I phoned the police and Sergeant Pepper came to see me post-haste. The young man was arrested and appeared in court some weeks later. I was called to give evidence, and this was the newly appointed County Court Judge's first case. I was cross-examined by the Sri Lankan's barrister. "Was this doctor not a very brilliant doctor". I replied emphatically "No". In court there were representatives of the Glasgow professorial medical unit, Southampton medical school and Pinderfields Hospital in Wakefield. They all had a lot of egg on their faces and were very anxious about their role in this man's long-standing deceit.

The young man in the dock had a large briefcase full of documents and produced one after the other when requested to do so but all appeared to be photocopies. The judge, by now irritated, told the court he would feel refreshed if just one original document could be produced by the defendant, who then explained that all his original documents had been unfortunately lost at sea! The British police meanwhile had been in touch with their opposite numbers in Colombo but had apparently not filled in the right forms so could not establish with certainty whether the defendant was qualified or not. However, Sergeant Pepper had managed to obtain an original document listing the names of graduates of Colombo medical school for the year the defendant had indicated he had graduated, and his name was not on this list. The young man was given an 18 month prison sentence.

Postscript:

Lessons were said to have been learnt by our personnel department and in particular never to rely on photocopies and the importance of original documents.

This young man was only rumbled because I did a one-to-one ward round. Elsewhere I am sure he was protected by his young peers, but it is frightening to think that he worked as a senior house officer in general medicine for one year without arising any suspicions. Moreover, his boss at that time had given my senior colleague a good reference. References should be treated with high degree of scepticism. An outstandingly good reference is one way of getting rid of someone who is no good. His use of night sedation kept problems quiet at night.

I reflected that some years earlier whilst a group of us were training as medical students in casualty that we were joined by a young man wearing a white coat. He worked alongside us apparently dealing with minor problems. Then he disappeared and we saw him next as we were doing our psychiatric training at a local mental hospital. We would arrive for a psychiatric teaching session at nine in the morning and patients with various psychiatric problems were then demonstrated. We were horrified to see that the young man who had joined our group in a white coat, pretending to be a medical student was not. The psychiatrist who had this patient's IQ measured found that it was less than 80. It is amazing what you can get away with in hospital even with a very low IQ!

This is an ever-present potential problem for our colleagues in management. Management culture encourages empire building with more and more managers, but care is always taken that any new appointees will not be a threat to the existing hierarchy. I personally have had experience of this phenomenon. We had a chief technician; he was a rock in our department and organised everything but sadly came to retirement age. We asked for a replacement, but we were told by the hospital management that we needed a departmental manager not a chief technician. We argued our case strongly, but the cancer of over management was spreading fast throughout the NHS and without informing the three consultants in our department a manager was appointed.

Some days later a spotty youth in a bomber jacket and rings in his ears appeared and told me he was our new manager. I welcomed him and asked about his previous managerial experience. "Oh," he replied, "it's quite good. I have done a two week course!"

This is in the days before IT began to transform society and medicine in particular. Our departmental library was the nerve centre of our department, a vital reference point and a space where you could discuss problems with colleagues. It was definitely important in patient care. However, all the doctors in our department were kicked out of the library to give our new manager some space. He went on to do virtually nothing. He was so bad and ineffective it was not surprising he was soon promoted. He could well be a chief executive officer (CEO) by now!

I developed a laser service in Leeds General Infirmary mostly for people with port wine stains in the UK. Patients came from all over the UK and some from abroad and the referring hospital trusts paid for their treatment on what was called an extra-contractual basis. This became very lucrative for my hospital and my part-time secretary had no problems in making sure all the income generated came back to our Trust.

Then one day I was informed I needed a laser manager. "Why not appoint my part time secretary." I said. No, the new manager had to be an addition to the ever-expanding management team. A young woman was appointed with no reference to me. Her salary was at least twice what the average staff nurse was getting at that time. She came to introduce herself and I said if she had any problems to let me know. Two days later she knocked on my door saying she had a problem. I said , "Tell me about it." "Rotherham?" she said. "Is it in Wales?" I said "I thought it probably was" even though it was just thirty miles down the road. She was so hopeless that she was rapidly promoted to become second in charge of computerising Leeds General Infirmary and more than 30 years later I gather that this is still a work in progress- no doubt fake news!

Back to the doctor imposter, shortly after the Sri Lankan went to jail, my senior colleague received a phone call from Sri Lanka. It was the young man's father in great distress. He had just received a call from a friend of his son saying his son was dead. On reflection I think this lad had struggled to study medicine in Colombo, where standards are very high and to avoid shame and disappointment for his medical family, he got a job as a technician in Glasgow. He used headed note paper from the professorial department to gain a place to study for a PhD at Southampton University. He was later told by the department there that he was not quite good *enough for a PhD but would be allowed to do an MSc (Master of Science) a lower valued degree. It is likely that at this stage he used Southampton medical school letterheads to apply for a general medical job and that he also borrowed a GMC certificate to forge, what looked like his own. I think because he was then in jail, he could not face his family and it was then he decided to ask his friend to inform his family he was dead.*

A CHINESE NEUROSURGEON

I arrived at Leeds General Infirmary in April 1969 and never had the pleasure of meeting this particular Chinese neurosurgeon. I was told that he had been trained by Willie Henderson, one of the consultant neurosurgeons in Leeds and had a very good reputation for his surgical ability and dexterity. He did however, have some eccentricities, but these were forgiven because of his surgical expertise. He used to carry for instance a lumbar puncture needle in his white coat lapel and used this needle to undertake diagnostic lumbar punctures if and when he thought it necessary. It is vital that no infection is introduced into the nervous system during a lumbar puncture procedure, but this fact seemed to be ignored by this man.

It was customary that speakers from all over the world would be invited to the neurosurgical department to give lectures and on one occasion the professor of neurosurgery, I think, in Vancouver was invited. This created a problem for the Chinese doctor because his CV stated that he had graduated and received all his training in Vancouver. Sadly, this was not true. The Chinese neurosurgeon had a lot of medical friends in the LGI and held a party at his house. He gave almost everything he had away and disappeared never to be seen again.

All this all took place before I arrived at the LGI, and I had no idea whether any in-depth investigation took place into this man's appointment and work.

A SPANISH DOCTOR

Pat was a hairdresser, and her children were at school at the same time as my children in Leeds. Her husband died very sadly of a type of leukaemia. Sometime after this during a holiday in Spain, she met, and later fell in love and married a Spanish doctor who came to live with her in Leeds. Pat knew me and also a colleague of mine, Adrian who was a consultant physician at Chapel Allerton and St James's Hospitals. She asked if her husband could join us on either our ward rounds or outpatient sessions as he wanted to sharpen up his medicine and try and practise here in the UK. Neither Adrian nor I were impressed with his medical knowledge, and he seemed very reticent about taking steps to become registered with the GMC. He became a patient of mine with minor skin problems but after two years or so of marriage he left Leeds for Spain. We learnt later that in reality he was an importer and exporter of fruit and vegetables and to his credit he never tried to practise. He just wanted to impress Pat by claiming he was a doctor. It was unfortunate for him, but fortunate for Pat that she had some medical friends, so he was soon rumbled.

Postscript:

Buyer beware is a useful aphorism. Original documents are vital. Sadly the GMC is not in any position to check the validity of documents especially from medical schools springing up all over the middle and far east established mostly for profit by local entrepreneurs.

It is a concern that the NHS is becoming increasingly short of doctors and special vigilance will be required to make sure applicants from other parts of the world have valid qualifications. On balance, a few unqualified 'doctors' will slip through the net. We owe it to our patients to be vigilant.

MRS T

As you proceed you experience some time at least in most of the medical specialities. Obstetrics was a large and integral part of training and offered a 'hands on' opportunity, often for the first time to clinical undergraduates. We took part in two three month periods of residency, living in the hospital close to the delivery wards in a group of ten students at a time. Mostly we had to monitor variables such as maternal blood pressure, pulse, foetal pulse rate and the position of the baby (a lot of guess work was involved in assessing the baby's position in those days before ultrasound made the situation much easier). Labour was often induced using a 'pit drip', an infusion of pituitrin, a hormone manufactured by the pituitary gland which would usually initiate uterine contractions.

Each student was allocated a patient to monitor, then deliver and carry out any suturing after the delivery as necessary. I drew a very short straw. My first patient was a Mrs T in hospital for her tenth baby.

Mrs T was a member of a notorious Roman Catholic Gypsy family living intermittently in Scotswood one of the poorer parts of Newcastle-Upon-Tyne. Her family, especially the male members, usually had long criminal records and were well disposed to violence. Fighting with other gangs in Scotswood was a regular occurrence, and just before I was allocated Mrs T, two or three members of the family took exception to being shown the door of a nightclub in Leeds. They attacked the owner, as he left in the early hours of the morning, with an axe. They killed his Alsatian dog with the axe and left an axe embedded in the man's head. He was taken to neurosurgery at the General Hospital in Newcastle where the axe was removed.

Incredibly he lived. Three members of Mrs T's family heard about this and roamed around the hospital trying to find the man to finish him off. Mrs T reassured a rather nervous fourth year medical student that she expected no problems as it was her tenth child and her many previous babies had come out 'relatively easily'.

I spent all morning monitoring Mrs T very carefully. By the afternoon I was getting hungry and bored. I was brought rapidly to my senses when Mrs T farted very loudly – this was followed almost immediately by a fairly vigorous rippling of the sheets in the mid to lower bed area. I pulled back the sheets and there was the baby in the bed. I tied and divided the umbilical cord and went on to the deliver the placenta immaculately. Fortunately, Mrs T was none the worse for her bad bout of wind and both mother and baby seemed fine.

Now began a desperate race between Miss Kerslake, a powerful feminist gynaecologist and obstetrician and the Roman Catholic priest. Miss Kerslake was intent on sterilising Mrs T, who was not terribly bright but had agreed, but the priest was not happy. In the event Miss Kerslake won by a close head.

Postscript:

I had my leg pulled about this delivery not only by the medical staff but also by fellow medical students and the trainee midwives, one of whom I later married. This episode however made me decide that obstetrics was not for me – A wise decision.

JOHN STEVENS

It has been my privilege to work alongside some of the true giants in medicine and John Stevens was one of these. John graduated in medicine in South Africa and served in submarines during World War II, where he developed a huge affection and respect for the sea. He told me that should he develop any disease that would ultimately kill him, he would set sail and let the sea do the rest.

John worked as a general practitioner in the Suffolk seaside town of Aldborough and for several years served also as medical officer to the Lifeboat Service there. John was always an individualist and thinking doctor. Whilst many GP's become brain dead from the sheer volume of work they have to carry out, John was not in this category. In the 1950's and increasingly the 1960's, barbiturate habituation, addiction and death from overdose were all becoming serious problems.

John had a simple answer and was the first GP in the UK to instigate a ban on barbiturates as hypnotics and sedatives. He would, however, prescribe barbiturates for individuals with epilepsy because at the time there were no real alternatives. Many other doctors followed John's lead and he became famous amongst his colleagues for initiating this simple but much needed change.

As a medical registrar in Ipswich I met John once a week in a medical outpatient clinic. After the session we did together we would then go for a beer at the Greyhound a pub opposite the hospital. The leading consultant at the time was doctor John Paulley, a giant of a man both literally and medically. He had a particular interest in the relation between stress, emotional and psychological problems with general medical diseases such as Crohn's disease, ulcerative colitis, migraine, giant cell arteritis and coronary artery disease and much else. He was really the founder of modern-day gastroenterology when he demonstrated small bowel mucosal atrophy as a constant and significant feature of patients with coeliac disease, one major cause of malabsorption. Dr Paulley was an intuitive thinker and managed to persuade one of his colleagues at the Middlesex Hospital to do an 'open' small bowel biopsy. This early work led to the development of the Crosbie capsule, a device to sample upper bowel mucosa when it is in place having been swallowed by mouth.

Paulley published widely on many topics and was instrumental in making the clinical features of, for example, giant cell arteritis a potential and sudden cause of blindness and stroke better known amongst his medical peers.

Not only was Dr Paulley very distinguished in the medical field he was also instrumental in establishing Buckingham University, the first private university in the UK. Paulley had always been very interested in medical education and had a sabbatical visiting educational establishments in the United States. Following this visit he wrote a paper on proposals to improve education and medical education particularly in the UK but no medical journal, neither the Lancet nor the British Medical Journal would accept his paper, so he wrote a letter to The Times which was published on a Friday. I was having lunch with John Paulley after one of his very long ward rounds when the phone began to ring. Notables from all over the UK were encouraging the foundation of what was later to become Buckingham University.

Paulley, with his particular interest in psychosomatic aspects of disease, encouraged we juniors and John Stevens to carry out some psychotherapy, albeit superficial, during the outpatient clinic. His fame did come with some eccentricities such as his use of corticosteroids. There was even an apocryphal story that he had a pet bat and that he had put this small mammal on steroids because he thought it had arthritis – surely fake news.

Some of Paulley's patients had to really fight to get out of the ward and sometimes patients would die of other causes whilst on the ward. We juniors took the opportunity of John Paulley's holidays to discharge a lot of his patients.

One evening after a tiring outpatient session, John Stevens asked me after a beer, if I would like to do a locum for one of his partners in Aldeburgh.

Aldeburgh and the Suffolk surrounds were rather unique in the nineteen sixties. Eccentricity abounded. Benjamin Briten and Peter Peers were distinguished musical residents and both patients of John Stevens and there was an annual music festival held at the Maltings each year. The Maltings were built many years earlier on the instructions of a Mr Garret, a local merchant who made a good living shipping corn to London and then coal back to Suffolk by barge. Mr Garret used his walking stick to indicate, to a local builder, how he wanted his Maltings to be constructed, clearly not wanting to go to the expense of an achitect and there were no problems in those days about planning consent.

Mr Garret had a daughter, Elisabeth, who became the first bona fide female doctor to practise in the UK. Whilst a male could purchase a medical degree in the latter part of the nineteenth century for fifty guineas no medical school would admit a woman and Elisabeth had to take her medical degree in Paris. This was after she was allowed to tread the wards of the Middlesex Hospital as an observer and not as a medical student or nurse. Not only was she the first female doctor in the UK, she was also the first female Mayor in England marrying Mr Anderson and the Elisabeth Garret Anderson Hospital in London was named after her.

Aldeburgh and its environs was a popular area for military and ex-senior civil servants to retire. Colonels were ten a penny and there was a healthy population of Admirals, Generals and even an Air Commadore or two. It was not surprising that alcoholism was a major problem. One Colonel would ring the surgery when he had run out of money for booze speaking only one word before putting the phone down 'Alcohol.' A home visit was indicated, and it was an art form reaching his bed through scores of empty bottles scattered on the bedroom floor. Another alcoholic patient filled his empty whisky bottles with urine to try and convince his medical advisors that he had given up the demon drink. Suffolk was also popular with well-paid high flying company directors who enjoyed sailing and a quiet weekend away from London in their Suffolk summer houses. One managing director, after a bitter row with his wife, used to release his anger in a particular way, donning some of his wife's clothes and sailing his ocean going yacht up to the Arctic circle and back.

The annual musical festival was a busy time for the practice when it was almost certain that one prima donna or another would contact the surgery because of loss of voice. The festival was well attended, and this generated many more both mundane and unusual problems. The partnership of doctors worked in a very traditional family practice. All the patients and families were well-known to their medical practitioners. Home visits were commonplace, and it was not unknown for one or more of the doctors to deliver milk or essential shopping to ill or frail patients at home. There were no problems with continuity of care. Suffolk had for centuries been involved in smuggling. If you were judged to have done well for a family, it was not unusual to find a bottle of brandy on your doorstep the following morning.

Everything seemed to be going so well for John Stevens and he was invited to give prestigious lectures and appointed visiting professor to many medical schools around the world including some in Africa where sadly his wife was killed in a road traffic accident. He knew Christian Barnard, the first surgeon to perform a heart transplant and told me that Barnard's sister was a girlfriend of his many years ago. From time-to-time John would drive a beautiful old Alvis car, willed to him by a London surgeon who stipulated he could have the car as long as John opened his radial arteries after his death to confirm that status.

John was slim, fit and active and a strict vegetarian, but he did enjoy a small cigar particularly after one of Dr Paulley's exhausting outpatient sessions. I was very surprised therefore to learn a few years after I had left Suffolk that John Stevens had suffered a severe stroke on his dominant side which had left him unable to talk. Despite this devastating and profound disability, John tried to continue practising writing questions down for the patient with his non-dominant hand. Understandably this was very slow and laborious work and eventually his partners persuaded John to retire from medicine.

John therefore started a new project reflecting his love of the sea and designed an ocean-going yacht that he, a hemiplegic and aphasic man would be able to sail single-handed. The boat was built and John set sail single-handed from Aldborough crossing the Atlantic and making land in Antigua, in itself an incredible feat for a man with such severe disabilities. There he wrote the last letter he was ever to write to a friend of his Basil in South Africa. I was to read this letter by chance many years later.

I had been invited by Professor Norma Sachs to give a series of lectures in Cape Town during the Annual Meeting of the South African Dermatological Association held at the beautiful Mount Nelson Hotel. This was in the days of apartheid. Norma worked at Groote Schuur Hospital and together with the professor of medicine, despite apartheid, insisted that their wards were multi-racial – a very brave stand in those difficult days. Norma was married to a GP, Basil, who had a very interesting practice in that he looked after many of the white politicians and also members of the African National Congress (ANC) at the time (including Nelson Mandela who was in jail on Robben Island and suffering from tuberculosis)

My wife and I were invited to Betty's Bay a summer house which Norma and Basil enjoyed for a couple of days after the meeting. Norma had some post conference commitments in Cape Town so Basil drove my wife and I down to their seaside resort. During this car journey I got talking to Basil and I told him that I had done a bit of GP locum work. "Where" he asked. I replied "Gateshead, Rothbury, Sheffield and Aldborough". Basil said to me that he knew a GP in Aldborough, John Stevens as they had been at medical school together and the last letter John was known to have written was to his best friend Basil from Antigua. Basil told me that John set out from Antigua but had encountered a storm, so he returned to port. Some days later he left Antigua again but was never to be seen again. John had always wanted his life to end at sea.

The South African Medical Journal published a special edition devoted to John Stevens and his last letter was published on the outside cover of this Journal. What a small world we live in and what a coincidence I should learn more about my colleague in this way.

Postscript:

John's initiation of a ban on barbiturate prescribing saved both many lives and much misery. Barbiturates used to be used by patients taking an overdose. More often than not, these individuals did not really want to kill themselves but merely wanted to indicate to the world and their family the problems they were experiencing. Many of the barbiturates were very long acting and in the bad old days therefore many people, often young, died unnecessarily. Barbiturate addiction was also a huge problem.

John showed enormous courage in life, and I am sure when the family waved him goodbye from the quayside in Aldborough, they knew what he was doing and that they would never see him again. It must have been a moment of immense sadness for his family, colleagues and friends as his yacht disappeared over the horizon.

Sadly, the availability of Benzodiazepines came to supersede barbiturates but on the whole patients taking an overdose of one of this group of drugs, were usually easier to resuscitate than a patient with a barbiturate overdose. However, death following a Benzodiazepine overdose can be difficult to establish with certainty, a point which should be remembered before stopping all attempts to save life and sending the body to the mortuary

Ironically one figure who actively promoted Benzodiazepines was Arthur Sackler, who later went on to promote OxyContin, a morphine analogue in the USA and thought even now to be responsible for 50,000 deaths in the States each year.

THE DEVIL'S GRIP

It was the summer 1971 when I was on holiday and so were my three daughters. I took them to a small museum near Kirkstall Abbey in Leeds and as we came out my eldest daughter suddenly stopped in the middle of the road and refused to move. She was gripped by a severe chest pain, and I had to carry her to the car. By the time I got her home, her chest pain had eased but she was mildly febrile. During the following week her two younger sisters developed a similar clinical picture. Out of curiosity, I sent off throat swabs and faeces for virological examination, more out of interest than anything else, and all three of my daughters recovered completely within a week.

Then it was my turn. I also developed severe chest and muscle pain and a low-grade fever. I felt dreadful. I also sent specimens for virology and the answer came back that we had all been infected by an enterovirus (a virus that lives in the gut) Coxsackie B2 which had caused us to develop Bornholm disease. This infectious disease was first described on the Island of Bornholm in the Baltic Sea hence its name. A local Wensleydale GP, Dr Will Pickles, had also written about the clinical features and epidemiology of this infectious disease whilst he was working as a GP in Wensleydale. After a few days in bed, I took the girls to Flamingo Park for the day. It was a very hot day. The girls appeared to have recovered completely but I felt rotten. Towards the late afternoon I developed severe headache with neck stiffness all thought to indicate central nervous system involvement by my GP and an infectious disease consultant.

My muscle pain and weakness persisted. Just walking a few yards was a real effort. I could not manage to walk ten yards to the end of the road to post a letter. In retrospect I think this was post-viral ME and very similar to the symptoms developed by a significant number of patients after Covid 19 infection – long Covid.

Two days later I had two episodes of left ventricular failure manifest by severe shortage of breath as I lay flat in bed at night. I had developed a cardiomyopathy as a further feature of my Coxsackie infection. During the episode of breathlessness, I was convinced I was going to die. I flung open the window to try and breath more easily. However, I survived.

It is interesting in those days that not a lot was known about Coxsackie B2 but I gather it has been recognised as a major cause of cardiomyopathy now in South Africa. I was off work for about six weeks. My consultant bosses were not happy – all my conventional investigations were normal. There was as strong feeling that I was just swinging the lead. However, I felt weak and generally ill and was still struggling to walk very far but I agreed to go back to work on a part-time basis but found in no time, I was working full time. To crown it all the medical staff departed for a North of England dermatological society meeting in Sheffield leaving me to do three afternoon clinics all on my own. I saw more than one hundred patients that day after which I was totally exhausted.

A few days later I developed orchitis (inflammation of the testis) but just on the left side. My left testis was very inflamed and walking was extremely painful. The inflammation gradually settled over ten days but I am left with a rather atrophic left testis as a lasting testament to this clinical complication.

It is interesting that the word testicle, testis, testament, testimonial and testing are all linked by the same Latin root. Apparently in medieval Europe a female called Joan was appointed as Pope, but this appointment only lasted a few months. Following this a special chair was constructed with a circular hole in the seat. Any new appointee as Pope had to sit on this seat naked from the waist downwards whilst one of the surrounding Cardinals checked for the presence of testicles through the hole and then testified that all was well.

I still experience muscle pain everyday more than 50 years later but have learned to ignore this (long Coxsackie B2).

Postscript:

This was the first time I had been acutely ill since childhood. I'd crossed that line that divides doctors from patients and became 'the enemy'. I found communication between myself and my various doctors very difficult and not very reassuring. The infectious diseases consultant was the most helpful as he explained that he had had Bornholm disease in the past but without all my complications. The cardiologist was completely negative but nowadays he would have recognised that Coxsackie B2 infection is a common cause of cardiomyopathy.

No doctor should be without an acute episode of illness in his or her life. I recognise doctors can be difficult to treat and one of the nicest things to see in an obituary where on the whole, pleasant things are written about doctors is that 'he was a doctor's doctor'. For me, like many people suffering from long covid, my symptoms were very real, but I recognise it may be difficult for others to accept a patient is ill when all the available tests are normal. As doctors it is important, we must differentiate between illness and disease. You can be ill with no evident disease and vice versa.

I wrote myself up in the Lancet under the heading of 'The Devil's Grip'. Subsequently I received letters from all over the world detailing clinical problems following an episode of acute chest pain similar to mine. For instance, physicians in New York had even suggested to an opera singer that she should have her pericardium (the sac around her heart) removed. I urged her to wait for that great healer, time, to intervene eventually on her behalf.

Several colleagues in my hospital developed acute Bornholm disease with some add-ons similar to mine and I was detailed to reassure them. The doctors involved included a heart surgeon and two anaesthetists and, in all instances, there were marked symptoms for many months afterwards. The extreme fatigue and other symptoms found in patients with long covid are becoming recognised as a complication of a viral infection especially in young and middle-aged adults. My three children all recovered within a week with no complications.

There will be some patients with long covid who will feel rejected by their medical advisors because they have no abnormal tests. I am pleased to say that a test is being developed to identify patients with long covid. I hope this experimental work will come to fruition.

Yvonne

Yvonne consulted me privately on a sunny summer Saturday morning. She was a teacher and mother of two young children, and married to a police officer. She was pretty, very well dressed and well spoken. Her complaint was that any cosmetics she applied to her face produced a burning feeling and her facial skin had become red or sore as a result.

I took what I thought was a full history from Yvonne and there appeared to be no other problems in her life. From her history I was expecting to make a diagnosis of a contact dermatitis to one or more of Yvonne's cosmetics but on examination her facial skin, despite her history, was absolutely normal. Here then was the paradox – a patient complaining bitterly about her face but there were no abnormalities on examination.

In the face of uncertainty doctors usually resort to tests and I was no exception. I asked Yvonne to bring all her cosmetics to the skin department on the following Monday so I could carry out some appropriate patch tests to detect any allergies she may have.

Yvonne attended for a patch testing on the Monday, and I arranged to see her to read the patch tests two days later. I finished my NHS clinic on the Wednesday morning and then waited for Yvonne who had arranged to come and see me at lunchtime, but she failed to arrive. She had in fact made me late for my afternoon clinic in Harrogate. I have to confess I was just a little bit angry about the situation, but my anger was to turn to astonishment when shortly after I began my afternoon clinic Yvonne's GP rang me to say that she would not be coming to see me. "Why?" I asked. "What have I done to upset her?" "Nothing." he replied. He then related to me what had happened. On the Wednesday morning Yvonne had telephoned her husband to ask him to pick up the children from school as she was going to visit her mother in Hull. Yvonne travelled by train from Leeds but got off the train halfway to Hull at Selby. She then went for a walk along the railway track and threw herself under the next passing train. She was killed instantly.

I was stunned by this news. I felt a total failure but on reflection Yvonne had not given me much chance to help. She appeared so well composed but this calm exterior must have been hiding a mind in turmoil. Her GP told me later Yvonne's husband had been having an affair and this was the cause of her suicide in his view.

Postscript:

It is recognised that skin disease can cause psychological problems such as anxiety and depression and also that psychological problems can lead to skin disease and exacerbations of existing skin disease. The association of a multiplicity of skin symptoms coupled with a negative examination was a situation that was new to me. My eyes were opened by Yvonne, and I began to see other patients with this combination. I gave these patients a label of dermatological 'non-disease'. I carried out psychological testing and patients with dermatological non-disease scored very highly on depression inventories. Suicidal ideation was also very common as was anger. I published a paper on dermatological non-disease and also began giving lectures on this condition. Colleagues began telling me about similar patients some of whom had committed suicide and if so, they often did it in a spectacular way. For instance, one woman set fire to herself with petrol. Patients with dermatological non-disease are profoundly ill not because of any skin problems or perceived skin problems but from profound psychological disturbances. Dermatological non-disease was a body image problem and it was not unusual to find some of the patients had other body image difficulties such as anorexia nervosa.

Following one of my lectures on body image disorder at an international meeting of psychiatrists hosted by the professor of psychiatry in Birmingham, our host put some of the delegates on a mattress in the back of his old van and drove us to dinner. The drive was bumpy and took about half an hour. I was squatting next to Professor Peter Berner a professor of psychiatry in Vienna who observed in the Viennese Medical School there was a bust of Sigmund Freud next to one of Kaposi a famous dermatologist. In the bumpy van on the mattress Peter proposed we establish together a European society for dermatology and psychiatry, and he would organise the first meeting in Vienna. This society is still thriving more than forty years later and has been instrumental in making body image problems better known for generations of dermatologists and psychiatrists. I served as president for this society for four years and the establishment of the society is my tribute to Yvonne. She died tragically but I hope not in vain.

RACHEL

Rachel was a very pretty young woman of 23 referred to me by a colleague who had been asked to see her because of acne and hair loss – only there was no acne to be seen and nor was there any hair loss on examination. Despite the negative clinical findings, Rachel was convinced that her hair was thinning and that she had active acne spots and resulting scarring. Rachel had a body image problem which I had labelled 'dermatological non-disease' but earlier terms in the literature included dysmorphophobia and body dysmorphic disorder.

It was my experience, that patients with dermatological non-disease always took much longer in consultation than patients with straightforward organic skin disease. These patients obsess repeatedly about the same problem, which they can perceive easily, whilst a dermatologist from the patient's point of view must be blind. The problem is that such patients have a dermatological delusion – an unshakable conviction that they are ugly in some way. There is a spectrum, however, and at one end patients present with an overvalued idea whilst at the other end there is a true psychosis. A major problem during the consultation is that there is a huge gap in perception between patient and doctor which can never be bridged. Affected patients often have a pre-morbid obsessional personality which does not help. They commonly produce a mirror during the consultation which compounds an already true heart-sink situation.

Almost all dysmorphophobic patients are very angry; this anger may be directed externally at the doctor or internally with an ever-present threat of self-harm including suicide. Patients like Rachel rarely consult a psychiatrist initially as they see all of their problems in dermatological and not psychiatric terms. Indeed, they may become very angry if a consultation with a psychiatrist is advised by the struggling dermatologist.

Because of these management problems I set up a liaison clinic in the skin department where I was joined by a consultant psychiatrist and where we could see patients like Rachel jointly without any loss of face for the patient. It became very evident that my psychiatric colleague was much better at identifying potential suicidal patients than I was. These clinics were hard work and my colleague said he saw more real psychiatry in the dermatological liaison clinic than in his own! I took a careful history from Rachel who had had problems with an eating disorder five years previous. Three months prior to seeing me she had a termination of pregnancy and I wondered if her problems could be a sequel to that procedure and due to depression.

What I did not know at that stage was that Rachel had been in prison for attacking someone with a knife. I became very concerned about this information because Rachel came from the Middlesbrough area where a consultant dermatologist had recently been killed following a knife attack in his home.

I was between a rock and a hard place; I had a duty of confidentiality to Rachel but also a duty to society. Could Rachel have been the killer? After much debate with myself I contacted the Middlesbrough police without Rachel's knowledge and thankfully following careful investigation the police were able to rule out Rachel as the murderer. Incidentally sometime later a heavily tattooed man was apprehended for the murder. Apparently, he claimed he had been stimulated by the presence of a skull on the doctor's windowsill. The doctor had a special interest in palaeontology. The moral from this murder is that if you are interested in palaeontology keep your old bones out of public view.

On examination there were no abnormal dermatological abnormalities. In short she was a very pretty young woman. Rachel had a perfect skin and a lovely complexion and also copious dark brown hair with no evidence of hair loss. I explained to Rachel that I felt she had normal skin and hair but there would always be a gap between each of us in our perceptions of the reality of the situation. Rachel responded by producing a mirror from her bag and insisted on showing me what she thought were numerous imperfections on her skin and acne scars. At the time I was very interested in the relation between dermatological non-disease and depression and Rachel scored very highly on a depression inventory and also expressed strong feelings of suicidal ideation. Was it her profound depression that was modifying her body image perception or was it her deluded body image perception that was causing her profound depression? Because of the high level of score on the depression inventory, I prescribed an anti-depressant, but I doubt Rachel ever took the medication. She wanted something for her skin and hair and not a drug for her mind.

Whilst I was at work the doorbell rang at my home and my wife opened the door and there was Rachel asking to see me. My wife explained that I was at work, but she came into the hall where we had a large mirror and she started pointing out her perceived skin problems to my wife who told her she could not see anything wrong. At that point Rachel raced upstairs to the bathroom saying she would wash off all of her makeup so that my wife could see what the problems were.

Patients like Rachel are desperate for confirmation of their delusions but collusion with the patient is not a good tactic. Rachel turned up next at the recently opened BUPA Hospital in Leeds. She had a major tantrum in the out-patient waiting area and shouted she wanted to kill me. Because this private hospital had only recently opened, there were no security staff, but Rachel was finally persuaded to leave without seeing me.

Rachel began to phone me usually in the evenings saying she wanted to kill me. This was not an easy time as I knew Rachel 'had form' with a knife but also knew that two plastic surgeons had been murdered by a patient in Wakefield and a consultant psychiatrist had suffered the same fate in Leeds.

What should I do? I discussed Rachel with a local consultant forensic psychiatrist – a colleague trained to deal with psychiatric medico-legal problems. I hoped he would be able to section Rachel because of her undoubted depression and suicidal ideation. However, when he got back to me, I was taken aback. He had not seen Rachel personally because he feared for his life. He had instead talked to Rachel's mother and as a result had made a diagnosis of narcissistic personality disorder. Patients with a personality disorder at that time could not be sectioned so who would prevent this young woman from doing something really disastrous.

Would the police help? I phoned them and gave them the history, but they said if I was a politician, they might do something but otherwise they could not help. I felt in despair and meanwhile Rachel was not keeping any of her follow up appointments.

About two weeks later I had to go to London and catch a very early train. My phone began to ring at about one am. I answered. It was Rachel. "I am going to fucking kill you" she shouted down the phone and then hung up. During the next two hours I had five similar calls.

I had to give a lecture at lunchtime in London, so I had to catch a very early train from Leeds. I felt very tired after answering all the phone calls, but I left home in the dark and closed the door behind me. As I did so I heard a rustling in the bushes at the side of my drive and then a figure became just visible in the dark. I thought I must face this encounter head on, so I walked towards the emerging figure fearing the worst. As I got nearer, I saw that it was not Rachel but a postman taking a short cut through my garden. My relief was immense. The postman apologised but such was my relief I told him to feel free to use this route as often as he liked. A month later I read the local evening paper and the headline was 'Girl Dies After Throwing Herself Off A Block Of Flats.' Sadly, it was Rachel.

Postscript:

We live in a society where it is not always possible to prevent people from self-harm. Rachel was extremely angry, and she turned the anger that was initially directed at me, on herself. The fact that neither a psychiatrist nor the police would or could help, and that she did not keep any of her follow up appointments perhaps meant that her suicide was her only solution. I felt a total failure but what else could I have done?

LEN

Len was in his mid 50's when I saw him for medico-legal purposes. Prior to becoming ill Len had been a very successful single-handed businessman building up his business over several years with typical Yorkshire grit. He was married with one son. Len told me he had begun to itch all over about 5 years previously. He saw his GP who prescribed antihistamines orally and topical corticosteroids, but the itch continued unabated and if anything became much worse.

Len was then referred to a local consultant dermatologist who found some small nodules on Len's itchy skin. Because of the diagnostic difficulties, many screening blood investigations were carried out which were normal, together with a skin biopsy which came back with a definitive pathological diagnosis of lymphoma, a type of cancer of the lymphoid system known to cause pruritus in some patients. Len underwent more investigations including x-rays and body scans to see if there was any more extension of the lymphoma from the skin. All scans and x-rays were negative.

Len was referred to an oncologist and had to wait about a month for an appropriate appointment. Meanwhile his generalised irritation had become really severe and completely unresponsive to any prescribed medication. Len was sleeping badly and so was his wife because of Len's restlessness but she was also beginning to itch. Her doctor thought she was probably itching in sympathy with her husband. Meanwhile Len's business was beginning to suffer because of his lack of sleep and also because of all the time he was having to take off of work for the various investigations.

The oncologist told Len he had cancer of the lymph glands and would need chemotherapy over a period of six weeks. There would be several admissions to hospital and Len found the atmosphere in the chemotherapy unit 'challenging and depressing'. He felt ill for most of the six weeks and felt unable to work. He lost his business and so in addition, to his medical anxieties he became increasingly concerned about his financial situation. No money was coming into the home. At this time Len's son got married. Len had lost all his hair because of his chemotherapy and his self-esteem had reached rock bottom during what should have been a very happy family event. For Len the marriage was both a nightmare and a disaster. Shortly after the wedding Len was declared bankrupt adding to his concerns. He was, however, more concerned that his severe itching and the nodules persisted despite all the chemotherapy. What next?

Len saw his local oncologist again and was referred to an internationally recognised centre for chemotherapy in London. His biopsy result was reviewed by the London oncology experts and a fresh biopsy was taken from another nodule. All this took time and a month later Len was seen again in London and was told he had a different type of lymphoma which would need different chemotherapy, and this could be arranged for him as soon as possible in a hospital in London. This entailed six weeks of agony for Len with the added problem it was a long way from home so he had no visitors.

Len was reviewed by his London oncologist about a month after completing his treatment. He felt depressed and was hairless and still experiencing the most terrible irritation. Nights had literally turned into nightmares for he and his wife. More nodules were appearing, more scans were ordered, and Len was seen again by the oncologist who told Len that the only future therapeutic option was a bone marrow transplant. This was very serious and Len was 'in the last chance saloon'. This option was not without potential complications including death. The only good news was that Len could have this procedure back in

Yorkshire. Len was desperate for anything to relieve his itching. He felt ill after the last chemotherapy and had lost a lot of weight. His wife was also suffering from increasing irritation. Together after discussing the pros and cons, Len with his wife's support decided to have the bone marrow transplant.

Len was subsequently admitted under the care of a haematologist who had an old-fashioned ward sister who was proud of her Yorkshire heritage and called a spade a spade. She did not mince her words. She told Len to undress behind the bed curtains and then to get into bed. Ten minutes later she pulled open the curtains and closed them behind her. 'Let me have a look at you" she said with a broad Yorkshire accent. Pulling back the sheets and assisting Len to take off his 'jim jams'. "You've got scabies," she said and she was right! The ward sister saved Len from serious wrongful treatment and harm. He was completely itch free a week later with appropriate treatment and so was his wife. The nodules withered away.

I do not know the outcome of Len's compensation claim but I was very supportive of him in my expert's report.

Postscript:

Scabies can be either a very difficult or a very easy diagnosis clinically. For example, in the very early days of the infestation there may be no abnormal physical signs but only irritation. The classical skin burrows develop early in the disease when a tiny mite can be extracted fairly easily from these burrows clinching the diagnosis. In a typical patient with scabies there may be less than twenty mites present in the skin and the intense irritation is due to allergy to a protein present in the mite's faeces. Allergy to this faecal protein may take up to six weeks to develop and during this period the infested patient will be itch-free but still capable of passing the mite on to others by close personal contact. At the other end of the scabies spectrum is crusted or so called 'Norwegian Scabies' where the affected skin is just one mass of mites. This type of scabies can mimic other skin disease such as psoriasis and is a potentially big problem in geriatric communities where one infested patient can infest literally hundreds of other patients and staff.

One of my distinguished predecessors at Leeds General Infirmary was asked to see an elderly Jewish inpatient lady with a rash on her legs which looked a bit like psoriasis. However, a skin biopsy was performed which showed a severe mite infestation of the skin. This lady's mites lived on and nearly five hundred other patients and staff developed scabies including my distinguished predecessor from this one patient

UK dermatologists do not really get involved in sexually transmitted disease which is left to venereologists nowadays called urogenital physicians. Some dermatologists, therefore, may not be aware that skin nodules can be a feature of scabies especially when present in the genital area and on the scrotum in particular. However, if one of these nodules is sent for histopathological examination without an appropriate history a diagnosis of lymphoma may ensue, as the changes in the nodule induced by the mite resemble those changes seen in lymphoma down the microscope.

Over diagnosis, over investigation, over treatment are all increasing possibilities facing a patient in the twenty first century. As doctors we should all remember that one of the commonest causes of itch, is 'the itch', a synonym for scabies.

SCABIES DURING WORLD WAR II

Scabies in Europe tends to arrive in 30 year cycles but close proximity and massive movement of people can exacerbate the problem and this was the case in England and France in both the civilian and military populations in 1939-1940. It was established early in the war using conscientious objectors who were made to sleep on blankets taken from known cases of scabies that the mite could only survive for 24 hours outside the human host.

A distinguished dermatologist from Leeds General Infirmary Dr J T Ingram was 'invited' by the War Office in 1939 to head the dermatological services of the RAMC (Royal Army Medical Corp) and given the rank of colonel. At the onset of the second world war the dermatological division in the RAMC was the largest, a reflection of the high provision needed to treat skin problems that were encountered during World War I such as trench foot and also plenty of venereal disease.

Scabies became rampant in 1939 and thought by some to be affecting the fighting ability of our troops. Uniforms soaked in a scabicide were trialled but sadly the scabicide was intensely pruritic and only made the itching worse by causing an intense contact dermatitis. What was the solution? The following account is apocryphal and may not be wholly accurate; in short my account could contain some fake news. It was said Ingram had his uniform made by a tailor in Leeds and wore it on the way by train and then by taxi to the War Office in London. It was also said that there was a lot of saluting in the War Office when he arrived and then a lot of embarrassment because the tailor had given Ingram wrongly the rank of Field Marshall! Not a good start.

Ingram always taught that it was vital when treating scabies to treat the whole family not only the index patient at the same time because there may be members of the family with mites in their skin but with no obvious irritation. Rumour has it then that Ingram approached Churchill with 'a cunning plan' to eradicate scabies from the UK and the military in France. Ingram proposed a scabies night signalled on the radio when everyone in the UK and armed forces were to take a bath and then anoint themselves from the neck downwards and all over with benzyl benzoate an effective but rather irritant scabicide. Furthermore, rumour has it that Churchill rejected this 'cunning plan' and declared Ingram mad. In any event, whatever the truth of the matter, Ingram left the army early in the second World War to be replaced by a junior colleague from Leeds General Infirmary. I have seen pictures of Ingram in the RAMC mess in London taken in 1939 but no pictures of him subsequently so it could be that the stories have some truth. Whilst the cause of Ingram's early retirement remains obscure, he was however, a great dermatologist who went on to be appointed to the first chair of dermatology in England, in Newcastle. Ingram taught generations of young dermatologists. He was instrumental in bringing medical science into dermatology, so in Newcastle art and science in dermatology became essential partners.

Ingram married Dame Kathleen Raven, a former matron at Leeds General Infirmary during Ingram's time there; she subsequently became Chief Nursing Officer at the Ministry of Health. I was Ingram's last houseman. Ingram held a retirement party, but his retirement was never lucky. Halfway during the party someone came in and said President Kennedy had been shot. There was an almost total silence following this announcement and everyone left the party and went home.

Ingram had bought a nice house in the countryside but sadly found that this was at the end of a proposed runway at Stanstead. He also bought a holiday home in Malta at a time when there was a very left-wing politician running the country. This man was not well disposed to Great Britain or to the British, I think possibly because he had married a British nurse, so there were difficulties put in the way of UK owners.

Ingram sometimes used to announce on the grand round that he conducted once per week, that he was neurotic, and after retirement developed severe asthma which was treated initially in the North East and then by a former colleague of his at the Radcliffe Infirmary in Oxford where he underwent a tracheostomy. He was treated with large doses of steroids and as a result became very Cushingoid (Cushing described a syndrome where there was an overproduction of corticosteroids by the body which led to obesity and moon-face, a buffalo hump, hypertension, diabetes, gastric and duodenal ulceration and osteoporosis and much more).

Before retirement Ingram used to travel down to London at the end of the week and then travel back to Leeds on a sleeper with Dame Kathleen so that they could spend the weekend together. There was some speculation that Ingram's asthma was psychosomatic as a result of not being able to handle the formidable Dame Kathleen.

Ingram had two large similar portraits painted and one hangs in the Royal College of Physicians in London and the other at the British Association of Dermatologist's headquarters in Fitzroy Square in London. His family gave me a large collection of his letters and his papers, and these reside in the Thackray Museum in Leeds.

IVY

Ivy is my 82 year old sister-in-law and her daughter Helen asked her to look after her dog. Helen lived in the countryside and the dog was old and had a scaly rash scratching incessantly. Ivy took the dog to the vet and a diagnosis of eczema was made. Appropriate ointment was prescribed but the scratching and itching got worse. A few weeks later, Ivy began to itch. She went to see her doctor who said she had eczema and prescribed local steroids. The itching became much worse, and she found it difficult to sleep. Her sheets, bedclothes and 'jim jams' were becoming bloodstained every night. In desperation she rang her brother-in-law (me) and asked for advice. Many years before I was asked to advise on a similar situation on a Crufts winner and the dog's owners. All three had mange (dog scabies).

I wondered if this was the same situation here. The dog had spent some time in the countryside and mange is a fairly common occurrence in foxes. There is now a very good treatment for scabies, ivermectin, two tablets a week apart will solve the problem and messy ointments and lotions are no longer necessary. Dogs can be treated with ivermectin, but they do not always tolerate this drug very well but there are other alternatives,

The vet in Newcastle was not helpful one reason being that she was consulted during the first spike of the Covid pandemic. I contacted one of the dermatologists in Leeds who tried to facilitate contact between Ivy and a dermatologist he knew in Newcastle. At this time, because of the Covid epidemic, the skin department was closed. I contacted another of my former junior colleagues (then a consultant dermatologist in Blackpool) who sent a private prescription for ivermectin to Ivy. She took this to Boots and was told they could not prescribe the drug. She took it to another pharmacist who said they could prescribe it, but it would be £1,000.00! Meanwhile my eldest daughter went on the net and managed to get the drug from the United States at a cost of about £30.00 plus postage. Ivy took the tablet and a the second one a week later and for the first time in 18 months she was completely itch-free.

Postscript:

I could not see Ivy at the time because I was trapped in Portugal because of Covid and there were no flights back to the UK. The irony of the situation was that my middle daughter who runs an animal sanctuary had a supply of ivermectin but I only learnt about this subsequently.

Ivy's skin problems underline the fact that scabies can be either a very easy or a very difficult diagnosis

SUSAN

Susan was in her 60's, unhappily married to an academic who appeared very often on local television. She had a history of bipolar disorder and was an alcoholic. She was usually more depressed than manic and eased her misery and solitude with alcohol.

Susan suddenly developed a conviction that she was infested by insects and despite reassurance to the contrary was referred to Adrian a colleague of mine practising as a consultant dermatologist in Durham. Adrian saw Susan and reassured her saying "Don't worry pet, I will kill the little buggers". Susan's conviction she was infested was confirmed, in her eyes, by this consultation. Adrian could find no evidence of infestation and so made a diagnosis of delusions of parasitosis. A delusion is defined as an unshakable conviction. In those days the treatment of choice was with orap an anti-psychotic drug which even in very small doses, and in the matter of a few days, led to a complete cessation of the delusion. The difficulty is always getting a patient to take the drug as a helpful pharmacist would explain to the patient that orap was indicated for severe mental problems.

Despite this difficulty I recall one Nigerian patient who wanted to take one hundred tons of orap back to Nigeria so impressed was he about this drugs devastating power over insects. He saw a great market opportunity in Africa!

Adrian next met Susan in his garden - she was combing her hair over his dog trying to pass her imagined infestation on to the dog. Shortly afterwards Adrian's mother and then Adrian began to get abusive phone calls from Susan saying, "you are a fucking awful dermatologist." Worse was to come.

Adrian was giving a series of formal lectures on dermatology to medical students in Newcastle. The lectures took place at nine am and were held in a medical school lecture theatre in front of about 80 gowned students. During one of these lectures the lecture theatre door burst open and there was Susan who walked quickly towards Adrian and pinned him to the spot with a bear hug whilst rubbing her long hair as near as possible towards Adrian's scalp and body. The students cheered concluding, wrongly, in the event that this was an angry rejected mistress or girlfriend out to shame Adrian in front of the medical student audience. Adrian managed to escape Susan's grip and she fled. Adrian had had enough and referred Susan to me! It is difficult to know where eccentricity ends, and madness begins. People with delusions of parasitosis suffer from just one solitary delusion, the rest of the mind is usually entirely normal. In reality the mental problem just consists of one cloud in an otherwise blue sky. A pre-morbid obsessional personality is common and sometimes there may be real preceding infestation. The condition usually presents in people of the upper end of the social strata – doctors and especially psychiatrists.

Affected housewives become exhausted spending most of the day, and even a lot of the night cleaning and washing. Other members of the family may develop the same delusion known as folie a` deux. Their reaction to the condition can be extreme. A patient of mine, a rich businessman, discarded all his clothes including a suit changing into new attire daily. His wife became so exasperated that she smashed a flowerpot over her husband's head and drove the Rolls Royce out of the garage at some speed, but unfortunately forgot to open the garage doors before she did so.! When I saw this man and examined him, he said "You will not see any insects today". "Why" I asked, "They are all up my anus." He replied.

The best way to manage this illness is to admit the patient and commence effective therapy with orap before any 'helpful comments' from the local pharmacist.

I spent a lot of time talking to Susan, but she refused admission and any treatment with orap. She went back to Durham and soon afterwards got drunk in a local pub. The landlord asked her to leave, but she refused and urinated on the pub floor. She was again asked to leave but this time she defaecated in the saloon bar. The police were called and she was arrested and subsequently jailed in Durham Prison where she hanged herself.

Postscript:

Susan was a very unhappy woman in an unhappy marriage. You can only lead a horse to the trough you can't make it drink. Susan would not accept any of the lines of help, either Adrian or I tried. Like patients with dermatological non-disease, she saw her problems entirely in dermatological and not psychological or psychiatric terms.

Why could dermatologists not just get on with it and rid me of this infestation was the uppermost thought in her mind. Her perception of her problems meant that she saw dermatologists in the end as useless and psychiatrists irrelevant resulting in a gap in communication between patient and doctor that cannot be bridged.

The condition is fortunately very rare and exceptionally difficult to manage when the patient is a psychiatrist. I was asked to manage one psychiatrist and his family with delusions of parasitosis. He just walked out of the consulting room. More worryingly I was also asked to see a pilot with this condition, who continued to fly his aircraft until he saw me.

Delusions of parasitosis is a very distressing disorder for the patient and it is amazing that even a tiny amount of orap just 2 mg daily will correct this psychosis in many patients – 2 mg of this drug lies between madness and sanity.

BONFIRE NIGHT
IN DONCASTER, IN 1966

In 1966 I was appointed medical registrar at Doncaster Royal Infirmary. I wanted to know what it was like to work in a busy District General Hospital rather than a teaching hospital where I had worked formerly. There were two fairly newly appointed general physicians, an elderly paediatrician and a dermatologist who looked after patients in two adult wards and a paediatric ward. When I arrived, I was amazed to find I was resident and in effect 'on call' 24 hours a day 7 days a week and my housemen, both junior to me were allowed to be non-resident. Well, I was married too with three young children and after some discussion I was allowed to sleep at home rather than in the hospital.

I had bought a small, detached house in Bessacar about five miles from the hospital. The house cost £3,250 and I had a huge mortgage to cover the cost. My salary at the time was about £1200 per year. Life was very hard both economically and medically.

For instance, as medical registrar my duties included looking after about sixty male and female adults and thirty children. There were usually a few dermatological patients also on the adult wards. A lot of my work was in casualty, and I often had to deal with post-operative complications on the surgical wards. Initially there was no intensive care unit and nursing standards were really behind the times. Life was very arduous medically. However, there were some positive features. The hospital was run by a young hospital secretary and his two secretarial members of staff in conjunction with a matron and a strong consultant body. These were the days of the golden NHS, and the hospital ran on oiled wheels both to the advantage of not only patients but also staff. There were, however, some tensions. One of the consultant physicians was having an affair with at least one of the out-patient sisters. His wife left him with all the furniture, so he provided deckchairs in his private patient waiting room at home and he explained to his patients that he was waiting for new furniture. His colleague's 17 year old daughter fell in love with a much older male music teacher, and the gynaecologist debunked to Australia with his much younger female registrar leaving a wife and several children. It was a small hospital, and everyone knew what was going on.

One of the older general surgeons was rather eccentric and reputedly mean. He is said to have lost his testicles at a young age and there was speculation how this had happened with no firm conclusions. He was a member of the Territorial Army and medical advisor to Doncaster Racecourse. In earlier days many of the consultants let out their houses for lots of money during Doncaster Race Week.

This particular surgeon had a steam engine and an old Rolls Royce. He was seen from time to time binding up its exhaust system with orthopaedic plasters and if you were invited to his house for dinner there would only be one radiator active in the winter and this was in the bathroom. He would wear his army greatcoat for dinner. He used to operate in a pair of old dirty plimsoles that he was alleged to have bought from his gardener for 7/6p (about 38 new pence). One of his surgical houseman stole one of these shoes leading to a major investigation about its disappearance.

A newly appointed radiologist would spend his lunchtime in the pub opposite the hospital drinking beer and most of his reports following a barium meal read 'Only a limited examination was possible.' A new consultant anaesthetist arrived from Scotland. He appeared very competent and was instrumental in setting up an intensive care unit. He also started an affair with one of the hospital telephonists and later left his employment in the hospital suddenly because of problems he had with the General Medical Council and drug addiction.

Although the nursing standards were suboptimal surprisingly, the survival rate after a coronary in our medical unit was better than other very prestigious centres such as the Hammersmith Hospital in London. For a while we congratulated ourselves until the reason became clear. Most deaths after a coronary thrombosis were in the first 24 hours. Most of our patients were reaching hospital more than twenty-four hours after the event when most deaths would already have occurred.

Beds on the medical ward were always in short supply particularly in the winter when there were usually additional beds put up in the centre of the wards and even at times down the corridors. Most of the male patients were smokers and ex-miners and came in with exacerbations of chronic bronchitis complicated by pneumoconiosis.

I was asked to see a young 30 year old man, an accountant, on an ENT ward one evening. He had a high temperature and his chest x-ray had been reported as showing extensive pneumoconiosis – except he had never been a miner. In reality he had a very serious form of tuberculosis (miliary tuberculosis) and he died that night.

Against that background one bonfire night in 1966, I was working late in casualty. There were no unduly difficult problems but lots of mundane problems mainly drug overdoses, a common problem in Doncaster in 1966 (it was a rather depressing place at that time). Usually, the patients were unconscious and had a stomach washout taking care not to wash out the lungs instead of the stomach. To this end an endotracheal tube was inserted into the windpipe via the voice box and this could be left in situ if the patient's breathing had been inhibited by the overdose, and then oxygen could be administered very easily if necessary. The tube was held in place by a small inflatable cuff.

I arrived home that night at about 10 p.m. Most of the bonfires had died out and hardly any fireworks lit up the sky. There was, however, a strong smell of smoke. My wife and I went to bed, but I could not settle, I don't know why but I felt there was something wrong, and this feeling became stronger and stronger. I began to put on my clothes again saying I would have to go back to the hospital. I could not resist this overwhelming feeling. On the other hand, my wife was wondering if I was having a fling with one of the night nurses. This was not so! To this day my wife remains unconvinced!

I drove to the hospital not knowing what to do or where to go. The medical wards were in the central part of the hospital on the third floor. I got in the lift for the third floor and in front of me was the children's ward in almost complete darkness. To my left was the male ward and to my right the female ward. I turned right into the female ward and saw the nurse in charge was smoking at the central desk – not a good sign. She stubbed out her cigarette as soon as she saw me. I asked if there were any problems "None" she replied. I noticed there were some curtains drawn around one bed with the light on. I enquired who was behind the curtains "Just an overdose" she replied. "Is she ok" I asked. "Oh yes" was the reply. However, I went to have a look. The patient was a young woman, and her face was almost black because of oxygen lack. Someone had connected her directly to an oxygen cylinder without a reducing valve, so she was left to try and breath against the pressure of oxygen in the cylinder. When I disconnected the endotracheal tube from the oxygen cylinder and without any oxygen, she rapidly became pink. Without my intervention she surely would have died.

Postscript:

I only had one similar experience about eighteen months later. I was watching a chat show and an Illusionist/Magician I think called Chan Casnasta was a guest. He asked the host to take three cards from what appeared to be a new pack, and replaced them randomly in the pack. At no time could I see the cards, but I had an overwhelming feeling that I knew what they were. I told my wife and when all was revealed I was correct. Fortified by this experience I had a small flutter on a horse a week later and lost my money. I have never experienced anything like this event ever since.

I have worked with many doctors and nurses. Some have had tremendous intuition and clinical acumen and some very little. In this regard pattern recognition is important and it is recognised that the ability to excel at pattern recognition varies greatly between individuals. In specialities such as dermatology and radiology, pattern recognition is still a vital intrinsic part of diagnosis, but it is also important in all branches of clinical medicine. On balance pattern recognition is an important part of developing clinical wisdom and likely to influence intuition positively. As the clinician ages, clinical experience and wisdom play an increasing part in patient management.

Advances in artificial intelligence AI) and information technology (IT) apply to medicine and diagnosis in particular depend not only on how the computer is programmed but very much on pattern recognition. Will the robots of the future be able to develop intuition let alone empathy. Will a robot be able to improve its clinical performance as a result of increasing clinical wisdom?

My experience on bonfire night in Doncaster had nothing to do with clinical experience, clinical acumen or pattern recognition. What happened on that night remains unexplained and a mystery to me. I shall never know.

SOME UNUSUAL MEDICAL GRADUATES

Glover:

Glover, that was his surname, (I never knew his Christian name) was 18 years old when he began his medical studies in Newcastle. As time went on, he was seen less and less in seminars, tutorials and lectures so by the time we had reached our final year, he had all but disappeared.

Just before finals he turned up for a medical tutorial with the professor of medicine. He looked and smelt like a tramp. His hair was unwashed and dishevelled and unusual in those days for a medical student with shoulder length hair. He was unshaven and at the end of the seminar the professor of medicine advised Glover to go and see the professor of psychiatry. This resulted in Glover being given a diagnosis of schizophrenia necessitating his admission to the local mental hospital from where he took the written parts of the final examination and passed.

This situation created a dilemma for the examiners. Should Glover be awarded his degree? Finally, Glover was allowed to graduate but happily never practised medicine. I am told he worked initially as a taxi driver, but the last I heard was that was living with an aristocratic lady in some style somewhere in the wilds of Northumberland. This could be fake news.

Charles:

Charles was a bright young graduate from one of the many London teaching hospitals. At first there were no problems during his work as a medical houseman. His behaviour, however, became more and more unusual. For instance, he would write his history and examination, after clerking a patient in ever and ever smaller circles with a diagnosis in the 'bull's-eye', and in tiny letters in the case notes. The consultant physician went along with this strange practice rotating the notes round and round to reach Charles's diagnostic conclusion. Shortly afterwards Charles, during a ward round brandished a knife and stabbed a colleague. He was suffering from acute paranoid schizophrenia.

Postscript:

Schizophrenia is not uncommon with an incidence of about one in a hundred in the general population and often presents first in teenage or early adult life. It is now recognised the schizophrenia may be precipitated in vulnerable individuals by strong marijuana (skunk). Stress may also play a part and in this regard a life as a medical student and later as a houseman is not without stress.

Calls have been made to try and lessen both undergraduate and postgraduate stress. This is a laudable aim but a career in medicine is always going to be stressful. There have been some calls for a medical examination to be carried out before anyone is allowed entry to a medical school. However, this would not detect some cases of schizophrenia. The numbers now entering medical school nationally make a medical examination impractical in any event. I never had a routine medical examination whilst I worked in hospital. The time period involved was 1957 until I left the NHS in 1995!

Julian:

Julian was an intense and also very tense and anxious young man. About three months into his six month medical house job, I found him one morning perched astride the roof of the female medical ward. I coaxed him down gently and sent him home for two weeks respite. He later became a distinguished surgeon.

Postscript:

The elation of graduating as a doctor is very soon tempered by the severe stress encountered whilst working as a houseman. The problem is complex but basically the training received by a medical student does not equip him or her always to deal with the many problems that may present on the wards or in casualty.

For instance, in my first surgical house job, I had to put up 14 intravenous infusions during the first day. In those days the drip sets were constructed 'in-house' and were primitive to say the least. The needles were usually blunt, and the walls of the veins were often punctured by the metal needle left in-situ. Shortly afterwards the introduction of the 'intracath' was an enormous benefit, not only for the houseman but also for the patient. Up until that point as a student I had only taken blood from a patient once so my first day on the surgical ward was a true baptism of fire. You had to be a very quick learner if you were to survive.

The practice of medicine is still very much about managing uncertainty which may be somewhat less nowadays following the introduction of all the recent advances in medical diagnostic technology.

Most medical students are selected to train often without an interview having obtained good 'A' Level grades in physics, chemistry, biology and mathematics. There is no pre-training medical or psychological assessment about suitability for a career in medicine. Interviews have some drawbacks as it recognised that the interviewers tend to warm to individuals with personalities similar to themselves. Once in medical school the pre-clinical years were dominated by anatomy, physiology and biochemistry. Students with the required 'A' levels find little or no problems. All are perceived as safe and there is always a formula or a way to resolve any uncertainty or doubt. These pre-clinical subjects therefore are relatively stress free.

Then suddenly the medical student is faced during their clinical years at medical school with patients with symptoms. Doubt and uncertainty prevail. Immediately the safety of the student's education so far is challenged. For instance, has the child with abdominal pain got appendicitis or not? Is the rash in this baby due to bacterial meningitis? Is this man's chest pain due to indigestion or is he having an heart attack? How do you extract this pea from the young boy's ear?

Problem solving and pattern recognition become core activities but medical students in my day at least received no previous intellectual training in these areas which are, after all, an integral part of medical practice. As part of our training, we received no specific teaching on communication but learnt to take a history in a long laborious mechanistic non-focused way. Non-verbal communication, which is so important, did not feature in our teaching. I believe I was the first to teach non-verbal communication to Leeds medical students who thought they were coming to learn about dermatology and rather resented my teaching eccentricities.

During my career I brushed shoulders with many medical teachers including medical school deans. I used to ask them to recall what their first day 'on the house' had been like. To a man or a woman, the replies were always illuminating and the words, terrible, awful, frightening were typically used to describe that first day as a young doctor. "Then why didn't you do something about it?" I asked. A shrug of the shoulders was the usual response.

One big problem doctors have is that patients die from time to time but 'clever teachers' in teaching hospitals do not seem to have patients who die – they do of course but they do not like to talk about it because they regard this as a defeat for them especially in the eyes of others including students. This attitude lead to a denial of the many ramifications occurring before, during and after death which were never discussed with medical students in my day. Clinical lectures given by teaching hospital consultants then were more likely to be about how they delivered a patient from the 'jaws of death' rather than about medical mistakes, the dying and the dead.

Even today there seems to be reluctance to let patients die peacefully. For example, my 96 year-old severely demented father developed pneumonia after he had fractured his hip. I explained to his carers in hospital that the quality of his life was such that there was no point in any active therapy, and I hoped that pneumonia would be the 'old man's friend'. My sister agreed but despite this, expensive intravenous antibiotics were administered, and oxygen given with a mask which lacerated my father's face. It seems that the geriatricians and even palliative care consultants are still somewhat unwilling to let a patient die peacefully so inappropriate, extensive and often expensive last 'medical rights' usually ensue. Are doctors frightened by the medico-legal consequences of masterful inactivity? I was not able to see any of the doctors looking after my father and all communication was via the nursing staff. Proper communication with the family at this time is vital and in my opinion the wishes of the family should be respected.

Another source of stress for the newly qualified doctor occurs when he or she has to go alone to certify death in the mortuary and even worse at the dead of night.

I shall always be grateful to Julian for making me realise there was a problem in teaching, at least in those days, which was focused on other issues. The teaching we got as students were on subjects that were easy to teach and examine on. In reality the examiners were examining the examiners as well as the students.

Patrick:

Patrick was Irish and, like his sister, suffered from congenital nystagmus. Both were students at university at the same time and both were almost blind. Although Patrick was very bright, he was to be found most days in the medical school common room playing poker. He was very successful at this card game and rumour had it that he had made enough money to buy one of the first night clubs in Newcastle. What's more he bought a Jaguar car and managed to obtain an Irish driving licence. An Irish medical student friend, Sean, used to volunteer to sit beside Patrick when he took control of the car. Sean was not a driver himself and his role was to tell Patrick when to brake, when to turn and when to stop! This Irish combination of driver and passenger was inevitably doomed, and a disaster ensued when Patrick turned right a hundred yards too soon on the Great North Road and ended up in a garden on the wrong side of the road.

It was not surprising therefore that Patrick's medical student career was not without some incident. During an obstetric residency he was asked to repair an episiotomy (an incision made in the mothers birth canal to facilitate the exit of the baby's head). Patrick was diligent in suturing this wound but took quite a long time over it. When he stood up from his operating stool, he found he had stitched his tie to the wound! Patrick passed his finals despite his visual problems and his industry was awarded with a house job in cardiac surgery! Every houseman had to do some nights on casualty and when it was Patrick's turn, he could be seen making his way down the hospital corridor with his hands on the wall for guidance! There was inevitably some debate amongst the examiners about whether Patrick should be awarded his degree.

Postscript:

Had there been a pre-selection medical it would be very doubtful that Patrick would have been accepted to train as a doctor. On the other hand, should anyone severely disabled be refused admission to medical school. During one of my father's admissions to hospital I tried to communicate with a rather obese staff nurse but was told by another nurse that she was deaf and dumb. Apparently, this severe disability had not prevented her from becoming a state registered nurse and able to run a geriatric ward. I gather that there is now a young lady who is both deaf and blind studying medicine.

Sadly, I don't have any information about Patrick's future, but he could have found a niche playing poker or running night clubs or both.

George from the Sudan

George was a very affable loquacious, gregarious medical

graduate from the medical school in Khartoum. I met him when he was working as a senior house officer in orthopaedics. George was an unusually bright graduate and after qualification was chosen to work as a houseman for the professor of medicine, a position that was strongly contested by his peers. During his first week in this job, he was awakened in the early hours of the morning by a squad of soldiers who told him that he had to go with them to a prison in Khartoum. Apparently, each week several prisoners were executed by hanging and it was one of George's duties as a house physician in medicine to certify death. George told me he was prodded into the dark depths under the scaffold by the soldiers where he would find several bodies in a heap. They were always dead and for six months this became a regular weekly assignment for George.

George told me, Muslim men like himself preferred plump women, possibly because the presence of obesity indicated that the woman was not suffering from a wasting disease such as tuberculosis. In this regard George told me that buttock enhancers were on sale in Sudan but had a habit of slipping particularly if the woman concerned began to run and would then trail behind so that everyone could see what the real situation was.

Female genital mutilation was common and even today it has been estimated that up to two thirds of Sudanese Muslim girls are subjected to this horrific procedure before the age of puberty. They are taken by their mothers to an Iman who would carry out the procedure without any attention to the possibility of sepsis or haemorrhage. George said that the Imans often used rusty razor blades for the procedure which carried a significant chance of death from either bleeding or infection. Sadly, the resulting scarring in later life interferes not only with sexual intercourse but also with giving birth. Genital mutilation is now illegal in the UK and also in countries like Egypt and the Sudan but prosecutions have been few and far between and young girls of Muslim families in the UK are still taken by mothers 'on holiday' and are being 'cut' abroad.

George had a very pretty plump Sudanese wife who spoke no English but she lived in the doctors' mess. George loved the mess parties which were, held on average, once a month and before each party George told me he would sedate his wife with diazepam and then enjoy himself with the nurses whilst liberally lubricated with alcohol and whilst his wife slept soundly.

Dr Singh:

Working as a junior doctor is undoubtfully stressful and doctors employ various activities in an attempt to relieve this stress. Mess parties, alcohol and nurses all played their part in varying proportions.

The mess parties were funded by 'ash cash'. This was 'folding money' received from the undertaker after a medical or surgical registrar had signed the Part II of a cremation certificate. For many years this regular source of income was used in this way but latterly the Inland Revenue got wind of the situation and mess parties became far less frequent as a result.

Dr Singh had qualified in India and was in his early thirties and unmarried. His bedroom in the mess was immediately over the junior doctor's common room. Dr Singh was in the habit of relieving his stress in a very particular way. He would go down town on a Saturday night returning to the mess with 'a lady of the night'. The junior doctors on duty whilst resting in the common room after a long day on duty could always hear a lot of noise emanating from Dr Singh's room. In those days the beds had a metal mattress frame and the old bed springs were quite noisy. When Dr Singh reached climax, he would scream much to the amusement of those listening below. One entrepreneurial and imaginative junior tied a brick to Dr Singh's bed springs so that the brick would collide noisily with the floor over the mess ceiling generating a large clang with every thrust from the Indian doctor.

Following this bed adaptation the junior common room

mess was unusually full for a Saturday night when Dr Singh returned with his lady. He wasted no time and proceeded 'to get on the job' when the brick began to hit the common room ceiling. The noise became louder and louder and ultimately climaxed with a loud scream. The junior mess found it difficult to control their mirth.

Postscript:

This rather cruel act on a foreign doctor working in a foreign country might at first sight seem particularly nasty and even racist. However, in my opinion it was symptomatic of the pressure the junior doctors were under in that exceptionally very busy hospital. It was a way of relieving the tension and stresses the junior doctors were under.

Ian:

I counted Ian as one of my best friends. He was an incredibly gifted, caring and conscientious young medical student. He was so obsessional that he was always late for meetings and lectures because of his over-conscientious concerns and commitments to prior work. There were never enough hours in a day for Ian and as a result his Christmas cards, always written with an immaculate hand, used to arrive in early February. Ian and I took an add-on BSc degree in physiology and there were only four of us on this course – one a pure science undergraduate and three medical students. During this year I got to know Ian very well.

As part of this degree course we had to experiment on each other. For example, I was the subject of an investigation on the suppressive effect of anti-diuretic hormone (ADH) on urine output. I was given an injection of ADH and a litre of water to drink. My urine was to be collected every subsequent half hour. The ideal result was a stepwise increase in urine output as the effect of the ADH fell off. Sadly, I was unable to pee in front of my colleagues in this laboratory and I produced no urine for three hours by which time my bladder was bursting and there was no way then I could hold back the flow. I began to fill all the available measuring flasks but the volume in my bladder was such that these proved inadequate. To save the day Ian snatched a huge bowl from a very large mortar and pestle which I duly filled. Disaster then struck. Ian dropped the bowl. The laboratory floor was awash with urine and what was worse the bowl of the mortar and pestle broke and was very expensive to replace.

My tutor chided me and told me I was a completely unsuitable subject for medical research and I am sure he was right. Ian and I went on to qualify and both of us became house surgeons in the busiest surgical unit in our teaching hospital.

To say these jobs were very busy would be a gross understatement. Patients for routine surgery were admitted during the weekend when they had to be clerked and blood taken for routine tests and for grouping and cross matching. In those days, there were no disposable syringes and the needles and the sterilised glass syringes had to be put together and moreover the needle was usually blunt. Our unit was on emergency take twice a week and we also had routine duties in casualty. Moreover, we had to do a minor surgical list once a week and a bougie clinic to dilate the urethras of men with urethral strictures usually due to previous gonorrhoea. We were expected to assist in theatre with both the routine and the emergency patients and it was usual to spend long hours in the theatre and on the wards especially at night with the emergency patients.

Ian loved this work and the drama of it all. I found it all very stressful. During our undergraduate career Ian and I undertook an elective placement with Sean just before finals in Workington. One night we were both asked to accompany a very frail and elderly man from the hospital in Workington to the surgical unit in Carlisle which had better facilities to deal with his obstructed inguinal hernia. Ian sat in the front of the emergency ambulance and was given the privilege of ringing the bell manually which he thoroughly enjoyed. Meanwhile I was sitting in the back of the dimly lit ambulance keeping an eye on the patient who was well into his eighties. I got chatting and discovered this man had had a most interesting life. As a young man, he emigrated to the United States and became one of Al Capone's bodyguards in Chicago. He told me he was still getting a good pension from 'the organisation'.

During our house jobs it was rare for us to get to bed before 3 a.m. and we were expected to be fresh as daisies at 8 a.m. in time for work in the main theatre the following day. As housemen, we had no time off during out six-month stint apart from a holiday of two weeks at the end of the job. It was impossible to leave the hospital during this six months of toil.

One night Ian rang in the early hours of the morning asking if I would go and see a patient with a dislocated shoulder in casualty. Ian explained he was just too tired to go so I agreed to his request. I walked down the long corridor from the doctor's mess to casualty feeling pretty drained. Casualty seemed rather quiet, so I asked the sister in charge where the man with the dislocated shoulder was. She replied, "There isn't any such patient." I persisted saying Ian had asked me to attend. Sadly, in reality the patient did not exist, and Ian had become so tired that he was hallucinating!

The following morning, we explained Ian's problems to our senior registrar (one position below a consultant) who was less than sympathetic. He expressed his views that we did not know we were born and recalled his earlier life experience working in casualty in Oxford. Our senior registrar told us he was very busy one particular night and he had been working non-stop for thirty-six hours when a badly injured female road accident victim was wheeled in. Our senior colleague said he went on to examine this woman but was so tired he fell asleep across her. He woke up sometime later to find his patient had died!

Ian decided to become a surgeon and was appointed senior house officer in surgery at the Westminster Hospital in London.

This was not a very busy hospital at this time and some medical cynics postulated it was only kept open for those sitting in the Houses of Parliament. Ian found at the Westminster that he could take as long as he liked when operating and with his obsessional personality every suture had to be perfect, even if it meant repeating the suturing in the same area. He could take all the time in the world, and this suited him very well. Ian loved his time at the Westminster enjoying the hospital atmosphere and did not mind covering for colleagues during Christmas and New Year.

Ian drank very little alcohol and never on duty. One New Year's Eve it had snowed rather heavily, and Ian left the hospital in the early hours of the morning to drive his tiny and much-loved MG sports car back to his flat. Ian found that his car would not start, and he attributed this problem to the fact that the snow was so deep that it had blocked his exhaust. What to do? Ian was very good at improvisation and took his starting handle and rammed it up the exhaust rotating the handle around 360 degrees on several occasions to remove any obstructing snow. During this procedure he was tapped on his shoulder by a young police officer convinced he had found his first drunk on New Year's Eve – but happily he was out of luck.

Ian's next job was in a busy surgical unit in Oxford where suddenly he was unable to take his time over every operation – emergencies were pouring in. Ian rang me in deep conflict, and I said if he wanted to progress up the surgical greasy pole, he had to lower his very high existing standards and accept that not all his sutures would be exactly perfect. After Ian was able to do this he became a well-loved, highly respected, very conscientious and able surgeon in Boston in Lincolnshire. Ian and his anaesthetist wife Jill lived in a house opposite the hospital entrance.

Sadly, Ian died as a young man of a really wild prostate cancer that he battled very bravely referring to it as the 'enemy'. He was able to accept this burden helped by his very strong

Christian faith.

At his funeral there was not a dry eye and standing room only, a high measure of the esteem to which his patients, family and colleagues held him in.

Postscript:

The long hours medical staff had to work in those bad old days came at a price and those of us working in this sort of environment were potentially dangerous. However, morale was high and continuity of care excellent. You were part of a family usually led by two or three consultant surgeons, a senior registrar, registrar and a senior house officer. The nurses wore a proper uniform instead of 'sloppy scrubs' and made you tea and coffee to get you through the night. Eggs and bacon were available in the ward kitchens in the early mornings. The ward sisters were hugely experienced and on hand for advice - which they never held back from giving. The wards were immaculately clean because the ward cleaners were under the direct control of the ward sister. The matron was all important and could inspect any ward for cleanliness at any time without any warning. In short, these were the golden days of the NHS before endless management changes sapped the life blood (and the cash) from the UK health service.

The changes began in the early 1970s initiated by Sir Keith Joseph the then Tory Health Secretary in Margaret Thatcher's government and who was referred to by Private Eye as the 'mad monk'.

At the time I was secretary of the Leeds and West Riding Medico-Chirurgical Society when we had a very elderly Jewish president, Dr Ike Rose who invited Sir Keith to give a lecture to the society. There was as reception before the meeting and Sir Keith arrived answering initially various questions from the assembled doctors and taking notes apparently enthusiastically in a small notebook.

Suddenly, abruptly and without any warning Sir Keith walked to the corner of the room, faced the wall like a naughty boy at school, with his back to his assembled hosts. After what seemed like an interminable age, which in reality, was just over five minutes, Dr Rose and I approached Sir Keith. Ike said, "I think you have been working too hard Sir Keith." Our speaker returned to the reception without a word of explanation, as though nothing had happened, and proceeded to give a lecture on the management changes he had imposed on a very unwilling NHS consultant body.

One very significant later change for medical junior staff was the introduction of an EEC directive to limit working hours to 48 per week. This led to a dissolution of the 'firm' system which was replaced by a shift system including night shifts. Junior doctors did not belong any more they just came and went and did their allocated shift. They felt alone, isolated and continuity of care became a problem. Morale amongst junior staff became and still is at an all-time low and worryingly up to 16% of doctors qualifying don't go on to practise.

There are serious potential problems with night shift work which occurs during the circadian (sleep wake cycle) normally associated with sleep. It is known that between three to five a.m. thinking (cognitive function) coordination and mood all reach a 24 hour low. Moreover, doctors following a night shift are obliged to rest during the day (circadian phase) which is least likely to encourage sleep. Long-term this leads to chronic fatigue and sleep disturbance. More worryingly night shift work has been linked recently to occupational accidents, road traffic violations and accidents driving home, weight gain, diabetes, coronary heart disease and even some cancers (prostate, breast and rectum). Moreover, 70% of trainee anaesthetists report significant fatigue affecting psychological and physical wellbeing and 59% reported an accident or near miss when driving home following a night shift.

In the 'bad old days' the junior doctors all slept in the mess and so driving home was not a problem. However, now most doctors live outside the hospital and the doctors mess is no more. During a night shift there is little opportunity for juniors to take a break and even if there is, there is nowhere provided by most hospitals for this to occur. Some doctors have resorted to trying to sleep briefly in *their motor cars for which the hospital charges them to park. Some hospitals have gone as far as to provide blankets for the junior staff to use in their cars on cold nights but outrageously charge a fee for banket hire. Is there any wonder morale is so low?*

The shift system is clearly not working but the old system was potentially dangerous. We need some radical thinking to resolve the very low morale amongst UK junior doctors. The necessity of having to pay to hire a blanket will not help this sad situation.

Recently, there have been some moves in a small minority of Trusts to improve the lot of their working doctors. Some, with the assistance of covid unemployed British Airways staff, set up lounges rather like those available for business and first class passengers before a flight, except no alcohol is available. Just the opportunity to have a coffee with colleagues to discuss problems, is helpful. Coffee at night, however, should not be overdone as caffeine is associated with sleeping problems and may add to the difficulty of day time sleeping.

ANOTHER MAD MONK – FAME FOR A DAY

I met Bob as a student in my first year at medical school. Like me Bob won a bursary to read for a degree in physiology so I got to know him quite well and he remains a very good friend. At one of our year reunions in Newcastle some members of our year gave papers on a host of different topics – most to gain tax relief on travel and hotel expenses. Bob at the time was professor of renal medicine in Newcastle and one of the organisers of the post graduate programme and so was more or less obliged to give a talk which was on an obsessed ex Trappist Australian monk.

Bob's one day of fame began early on a fateful morning in 1981 at Dublin airport as he boarded an Aer Lingus flight for Heathrow. Bob had given a paper on renal disease the day before and following this he had enjoyed some excellent Irish hospitality which left him feeling, as he sank in to his second row seat, that he should have been more restrained with the Irish whiskey. In short he was feeling fairly wretched and still wondering how he had survived the taxi ride to the airport. He was encouraged by looking forward to spending a quiet Saturday afternoon with his wife and three daughters in the garden and even dreamt of cutting the lawn.

Once airborne the flight was hi-jacked by a crazy Australian monk and Bob had a ringside view from his second row seat. The monk who was holding a milk bottle containing fluid declared he had dowsed himself in petrol and demanded that the plane fly to Tehran otherwise he would set himself alight. His other demand contained in a 9 page document was the publication of it's contents in the Irish press calling for the third secret of Fatima to be revealed, a secret known only at the time by the Virgin Mary, the Pope and a Portuguese nun, then aged 74.

The pilot explained he did not have sufficient fuel to fly to Tehran so he would have land at Le Touquet . The mad ex monk accepted the captain's assertion and started intoning strange incantations. As the plane landed, darkness fell and one elderly female passenger declared she was feeling ill and with the mad monk's permission Bob was allowed to talk to her. Incredibly, Bob told me she had had the same abdominal symptoms for 20 years but nevertheless an ambulance was allowed to the steps of the plane. Under this cover the French equivalent of the SAS stormed the plane and the hijack was over. Amazingly, the French rescuers arranged a dinner for all the passengers and crew with plenty of champagne. I doubt that this would happen in the UK.

More recently the Vatican released the third secret of Fatima – it was that a Pope would be shot. Sadly this prophesy came true but fortunately was not fatal.

Bob for a day made the front pages of the The News of the World, a rather scurrilous newspaper. Bob commented to me that most doctors who attained this front page status usually had appeared before the General Medical Council for alleged professional misconduct. Some years later, Mr Murdoch, referred to by Private Eye, as the 'dirty digger' closed down this publication known affectionately by is devotees as the 'Screws of the World' following serious allegations of phone hacking.

FRIENDS

Gary:

Gary was born in 1940 and told me his mother hated him but doted on his younger brother Eric. Gary could not wait to get away from home, so he joined the British Army at the age of seventeen. He was very short sighted and not particularly athletic, so he became craftsman Wright in the REME and was posted to Aden. Whilst walking one evening Gary struck up a conversation with a British civil servant who complained that there was nowhere in Aden for people like himself to have their cars serviced. Gary, always the entrepreneur, said he could organise servicing in the REME workshop.

Gary was never well co-ordinated, and this led to him not being trusted in the workshop even with a spanner. However, his colleagues readily agreed to this extra work which would supplement their rather meagre army pay. As Gary was no use with a spanner, he was delegated by his sergeant to get rid of army surplus goods like old tents. He would load up a four-ton truck and drive into the hills. He would be followed by a group of Arab 'businessmen'. He took the tents and other redundant equipment out of the lorry and began by setting fire to some of it. It became immediately clear to Gary that there was a potential local market amongst the Arabs for this army surplus so he would burn a few old tents initially to get the locals interested. He sold the rest easily and this money helped Gary later to establish his early business interests in the UK. The car servicing business also thrived. His discharge was hastened by a near fatal motor bike accident in Aden and recovery from this took about a year in the UK.

Gary's first venture into his own business involved selling blankets door to door with his brother Eric in the poorer parts of Leeds. They tried Gipton first and set out in different directions in this estate and agreed to meet at lunchtime. When they met Eric declared that he had sold all his blankets. "How much money did you get"? asked Gary. Eric explained "None" but all the recipients of the blankets had promised to pay later. For Gary this was a disaster as the blankets seemed irretrievable. How could he get the blankets back as he knew none of the Gipton residents had any intention of paying later? However, Gary succeeded in retrieving the blankets by apologising to the recipients, saying he had discovered the blankets were radioactive!

Gary began retailing carpets and was very successful. He had married Iris and had three sons. He decided to splash out on a really different holiday in Europe. He saw a boat advertised in "Exchange & Mart" and sent his business partner, John Needham, down to East Anglia to make sure the boat was seaworthy and in good condition and if so to tow it back to Yorkshire. The boat arrived back in Leeds on a small trailer and Gary decided that he, his family and the boat would go on a holiday to what is now Croatia which was then in old communist Yugoslavia. Gary and his family set off but by the time they reached the Alps the tiny tyres on the boat trailer were threadbare and it took them three days to find anyone who was able to replace them. Eventually after more than a week driving with three young and combative sons in the car, Gary and the boat arrived at its destination – a small village on the beautiful Adriatic coast.

After moving their luggage into the rented house Gary towed the boat down to the little harbour and gave the harbour master, who spoke no English, a large cigar. Gary and the harbour master sat together in the sun, each smoking their cigars. Then the time came to launch the boat. Gary backed the trailer carefully down the ramp and into the Adriatic Sea.

The boat slowly sank!

After a few days letting the boat dry out Gary set off back to the UK with boat in tow. Gary was amazed when the Austrian customs wanted to charge him duty maintaining the boat was new! The tyres became threadbare again in the Alps necessitating a further three-day delay. Eventually the family and the boat arrived back in Leeds.

At the first opportunity Gary took the boat to a boat yard under the dark arches, close to Leeds central station. The owner declared Gary needed another boat and he had just the thing for him. Gary set off to Bridlington on the East Coast of Yorkshire with his new vessel accompanied by Eric his brother. The boat was lowered gently into the water and happily it did not sink. Gary and his brother climbed aboard and sailed out of the harbour into Bridlington Bay. The motor was working perfectly, and the boat gathered speed. Eric was at the helm and decided suddenly to try and put the boat in reverse. Unfortunately, there was only a small distance between the sea and the stern of the boat. This manoeuvre created a small tsunami, flooding and ultimately sinking the boat. Gary and his brother found themselves in the water. However, Bridlington Bay is quite shallow, and they were able to tow the boat onto the beach. The boat was duly towed back to Leeds and to the boat yard under the dark arches. "You need a different boat"' said the owner, 'I have just the job for you'. This was a much bigger boat on a much larger trailer. Gary left the boat yard feeling proud of his new boat. He set off towing the boat to his home in North Leeds. As he was proceeding up Burley Road, not far from the centre of Leeds, he was overtaken by a boat on the wrong side of on the road. Amazingly it was his new boat which had not been secured properly on the trailer. The boat collided violently with an oncoming Honda and both the boat, and the car were total write offs. Fortunately, no one was badly hurt. That was the end of Gary's journey into the maritime world.

Gary had a passion for old cars. Some years ago, he bought a beautiful Rover three litre convertible. The car was in immaculate condition and was a delight to drive. On suitable days Gary would take the car to special rallies with similar Rover vehicles. After owning the car for ten years or so he decided he wanted more room in his garage and indicated in a Rover owners' magazine that he may be interested in selling the car.

Sometime later he received a phone call from a man speaking in English with a heavy foreign accent. He explained he was phoning on behalf of someone else who would be interested in purchasing the convertible. The buyer said he would offer £25,000 for the vehicle. Gary readily agreed and said when the money was received by his bank the car could be collected. Gary learnt later that the Rover was destined for the car collection of the Emir of Kuwait and the man on the phone was the Kuwaiti Prime Minister. Gary had doubled his money in the twelve years he had had the car and was well pleased with this trade.

Adrian:

Adrian was born in the Northeast and became a consultant dermatologist in that area. He was very good at his job and was respected by his colleagues for his diagnostic and management skills. He and I used to exchange difficult patients such as Susan (see above).

As a teenager Adrian told me he had become increasingly interested in girls. For a special treat to himself, for his 16th birthday, he went to a dance in Newcastle where he met a similarly aged girl who indicated that they could 'get together' the following Saturday afternoon her parents were going to watch some mystery plays in York. The young girl lived in Gosforth, a very respectable and middle-class area of Newcastle and Adrian lived in Gateshead on the south side of the River Tyne.

As the Saturday approached Adrian became more and more excited. On the day in question, he could not sleep so he got up at 6 a.m. and cleaned his bike. By 8 a.m. he was cycling to Gosforth. It took less than an hour but seemed like a lifetime.

As he cycled along Gosforth High Street the shops were just beginning to open. He wanted to buy a packet of durex so optimistic was he about this new relationship. He found a chemist's shop in the high street and went in rather nervously. As he reached the counter a woman came to serve him, so he asked for a tin of elastoplasts. He cycled around for another hour and went back into the chemist's shop. Frustratingly a different woman came to serve him, so he asked for some panadol.

Time was getting on and he knew the chemist would close at 12 noon. In desperation just before midday he went back into the chemist's shop. Imagine his relief when he saw a man serving. Adrian asked for a packet of durex then left hurriedly. Some of his anxiety had abated and he felt on the crest of a wave.

He had arranged to meet the girl at her house at three o'clock that afternoon and he made several more circuitous rides around Gosforth but by 2.45 p.m. he could contain himself no more. He knocked at his new girlfriend's door. The door was opened by the girlfriend's father who invited Adrian in. He shouted to his daughter and asked Adrian if he liked mystery plays. Adrian replied in the affirmative and off the whole family went with Adrian by car to York. Adrian sat with his girlfriend in total silence in the back seat of the car. The first chance to speak was at the interval. Sarah, that was her name, was furious, "I told you to come at 3" she said and added "I didn't know you were interested in mystery plays." "I am not" Adrian replied but I didn't know your father had a chemist's shop in Gosforth high street either!" Life at times can be very frustrating.

Adrian became a popular lecturer both at home and abroad. Following a meeting he was a guest of Neils Hjorth, professor of dermatology in Copenhagen at his summer house on the Baltic Coast. The other guest was Ronnie Marks professor of dermatology in Cardiff.

Neils was a very good host, and all three friends drank much more than the present miserly recommendations of the experts who seem more interested in longevity than quality of life. In any event a good night was had by all, and they retired to bed.

In the dark early hours of the morning Adrian knew he had to get up to urinate. One little problem was that the bathroom was some way away down the corridor from his bedroom. However, it was summer, and his window was open. Still a little intoxicated with supressed inhibitions Adrian relieved himself through the window and repeated the process as dawn approached.

The following morning breakfast was on the terrace under a pergola festooned with bunches of grapes. Ronnie supplemented his breakfast with some of the grapes picked from the overhead vines. Ever the scientist and a keen observer he noticed some of the green grapes felt wet whilst other adjacent grapes were quite dry. How could this be explained he asked. Adrian wisely said nothing, saying it was all a bit of a mystery.

Adrian was a keen fisherman, and each year would travel to Ireland where he was joined by a medical friend from California. They shared a room in a small pub on the banks of the loch. They enjoyed a surfeit of Guinness on the first night and retired to bed a bit worse for wear.

Adrian began to dream that he was being whipped and told me that on the whole this was not unpleasant. Eventually he woke up to find his Californian friend beating him with a fishing rod to stop him snoring. Later whilst fishing in Canada Adrian observed dryly that when you fancied having sex with the squaw who had been doing the cooking, it was time to go home.

I had the pleasure of traveling to India with Adrian. We both had been invited to give some lectures as guests of the Indian dermatological society. We flew together from Heathrow one evening courtesy of British Airways. The plane was crowded, and we were in economy. Adrian sitting in an aisle seat showed me proudly a new leather money and drug pouch which I think he had purchased during a visit to South America and which he wore halfway up his left leg. After a meal about four hours out of Heathrow, Adrian said he was going to sleep. He reached into the pouch for a 5 mg tablet of diazepam and after taking this put on a blindfold over his eyes. 30 seconds later came a call for a doctor to go urgently to the back of the plane. Adrian did not move pretending to be asleep, so I had to go. At the back of the plane there was a hysterical Kuwaiti woman hyperventilating. I was attended by a very 'camp' steward, and I used a 'sick bag' for the woman to breath into. This cured her hyperventilation, but she was still obviously very anxious. I asked the steward if they had any medication on board. "No" he replied. I asked him to come with me. Adrian was asleep by this time, and I indicated to the steward that he would find some appropriate medication up Adrian's left leg. Adrian woke up suddenly to find the steward groping up his left leg. A diazepam tablet was extracted and given to the Arab lady and three- or four-hours later we arrived safely in Kuwait. Adrian was initially alarmed by what seemed to be the steward's very inappropriate attention but soon became cooperative when the circumstances were explained to him.

We re-joined the flight to Delhi. Just after the plane had taken off an announcement came over the tannoy system asking if the two doctors in economy would go immediately to the front of the aircraft. On this occasion Adrian could not fain that he was asleep, so we went to the front of the plane as quicky as possible. To our surprise we did not find an ailing patient, but were allocated business class seats as a token of gratitude for my help with the Kuwaiti passenger.

We arrived in Dehli and after an overnight stay the plan was to fly on to Calcutta where the meeting was being held. However, the flight to Calcutta was cancelled because of fog at Calcutta Airport. Adrian had made the arrangements for our visit and our hosts were going to meet us at the airport in Calcutta when the plane arrived. We tried to ring to say our flight was delayed but the phones would not work. As a result, we arrived very late in Calcutta with no idea where the meeting was going to be held and no idea where we were to be accommodated.

Adrian, always the entrepreneur, asked the taxi driver to take us to the best hotel in town which turned out to be the Oberoi Grand and we checked in there. We could not believe our luck when we learnt that the dermatology meeting was being held in the self-same hotel. Because of the delay in our flights, we missed meeting Mother Teresa who had opened the meeting two days previously.

Another colleague from Leicester had arrived on time and found himself accommodated in a local leprosy colony. We were also destined to be accommodated in this leprosarium. After talking to our colleague who was staying there who described the accommodation as rather rough, we elected to continue staying in the Oberoi Grand.

Adrian subsequently became very ill with gastroenteritis. His upper abdominal pain was so severe in the initial stages that he thought that he may have pancreatitis and the situation was so grave that he gave up alcohol. I took my own bottled water and lots of tins of spam but despite these precautions I also developed gastroenteritis which persisted after I got home. My daughters were very disinclined to use the toilet after me.

Postscript:

I think India is a bit like Marmite you either love it or hate it. The sites I experienced in and around Calcutta were unlike anything I had ever seen before, and I felt that one visit to this city was enough. Our hosts, when they invited us, had indicated that they would pay for our flight and accommodation. In the event we received payment for neither, I think because we stayed at the Oberoi Grand instead of the leprosarium.

The return flight from Calcutta wasn't without incident. We checked in after telling about 50 potential porters, who all wanted to help with our luggage, to go away in no uncertain terms. When we checked in, we were told that the flight was delayed by 6 hours. We asked if there was a bar and were told that there wasn't. However, we were informed there was a hotel about a mile down the road. We emerged from the airport building with our hand luggage. It was an extremely hot day. None of the hordes of porters who had previously wanted to help us approached us following their admonition by our colleague from Leicester. In the boiling heat we pulled our hand luggage one mile down the road to the hotel, wheeling our way around elephant dung. We found a bar and quenched our thirst and disappointment that our flight home was delayed.

We had to pay a departure tax of 12 rupees, and I told the man in the kiosk that this was the best 12 rupees I have ever spent in my life. Fortunately, we were allocated seats very near the toilets and our bowels were exercised on numerous occasions on the flight back to the UK. Shortly after arriving back at Heathrow, Adrian developed pneumonia but thankfully he recovered.

INNSBRUCK

In the 80's a new treatment for psoriasis was described jointly from dermatological units in the USA and Austria. It was called PUVA therapy. P stood for psoralens, a drug given orally or applied topically before skin exposure to a specific wavelength of ultraviolet light – ultraviolet light A (UVA).

Psoralens was extracted from a plant growing along the Nile and had been used since ancient times to try and treat vitiligo, a skin disease characterised by white de-pigmented areas on the skin. Great care had to be taken with this treatment as it was possible to burn patients badly if too much UVA was given.

I wanted to see this new treatment in action. Klaus Wolf (see Wilma and Klaus above) was then professor of dermatology in Innsbruck and was operating a PUVA unit there. I arranged to go and visit this unit for a few days and at the last minute I got a phone call from Dr Freshwater, an elderly and distinguished dermatologist in Liverpool asking if he could join me. I agreed and we arranged to meet at Manchester Airport some days later. In those days there were no direct flights to Innsbruck and you had to fly first to Munich and then take a train to Innsbruck. The flight to Munich was very early in the morning so I had to set off by car from Leeds at about 3 a.m. Freshwater was waiting for me at the Airport, and he proved to be a very agreeable companion. He told me in his younger days he had played tennis at Wimbledon for England. He was called up and spent the early war years in the Royal Army Medical Corps (RAMC) in Cairo with the rank of Major and was paid £650 per year. This he explained was a very princely sum in Cairo at that time. For instance, for 7 shillings and 6 pence he could hire a dhow with a full crew for a week and entertain nurses of his choice up and down the Nile. Dr Freshwater's war and hedonistic lifestyle came to an abrupt end with the Italian invasion and Freshwater spent the rest of the war in Italy.

We landed safely in Munich and took a taxi to the station where we caught the train for Innsbruck. Freshwater was not sure whether we had first class tickets or not, but the train was nearly empty, and we settled down in a first class compartment. Just before the train set off, we were joined by an Austrian and we started chatting. The train got underway, and the ticket inspector arrived and told us we were in the wrong part of the train. We were very comfortable where we were, so we paid him a supplement and continued our conversation with our Austrian companion who told us he was an architect. He asked us where we were staying in Innsbruck, and we told him we were staying at the Holiday Inn. "Oh" he exclaimed. "I was the architect for that hotel." Furthermore, he said he had an apartment on the whole of the top floor of the hotel which, if it was vacant, he was willing to let us occupy for the duration of our stay free of charge. "Just show my card at reception" he said. We did and his apartment was vacant – just as well as the money for my stay in the hotel had not yet arrived.

The apartment was huge with a massive central lounge with en-suite bedrooms on each side. Freshwater said he was going to have a shower and disappeared into his end of the apartment. I thought I may as well do the same. After 20 minutes or so I emerged into the lounge wearing a bathrobe. Freshwater was already sitting on a sofa also in a bathrobe.

As I approached him a look of horror appeared on his face. He was looking at my feet. A look of horror then appeared on my face. All my toenails had been painted red with nail varnish. Freshwater was obviously worried he had to spend a few days with a 'camp' Leeds dermatologist. I reassured him, one of my daughters will have painted my nails the previous night whilst I was asleep in the chair. A phone call to my home in Leeds confirmed this. Freshwater was reassured and we spent the next few days learning about PUVA. Both of us went home and set up new units in both Leeds and Liverpool.

Postscript:

Things are not always as they appear, and I suppose we all judge individuals to some extent by appearance and later actions.

A latent fear of homosexuality is in my experience common, more so in men, and this latent fear drives some homophobic individuals and some governments to aggressive action against the homosexual population. One aspect of personality - tolerance is sorely lacking in this world of ours.

THE YORKSHIRE RIPPER

The murders attributed to the 'Yorkshire Ripper' led to very unusual times in Leeds and to the doctors in particular. The investigational waters were muddied by a tape recording by a man with a Northeast accent claiming to be 'Jack The Ripper'. This tape was later proved to be false but led the police and the man in charge of the investigation in particular to believe the Ripper had Northeast connections. Thousands of men were questioned but most of the statements then lay in cardboard boxes with no attempt at correlation by computer. Two Leeds police officers were charged and convicted of trying to blackmail Jimmy Savile. At one stage the police had a theory that the culprit was a doctor. After all who could come home with bloodstained clothes with no suspicion. This thinking underlined police thinking at the time and I do not think I have known of any doctors coming home with bloodstained clothes. However, the police put a tail on one of my forensic pathology colleagues, professor Michael Green who was not involved in carrying out post-mortems on any of the victims. Mike Green delighted playing hide and seek with the police followers sometimes leaving his home via his back fence to frustrate his tail.

One day the police burst into my private consulting rooms at my house, whilst I was seeing private patients to ask me to do a 'bite test' and I was asked where I was on that particular night of one of the murders. My eldest daughter kept a diary and she read out that I had fallen asleep in the lounge whilst watching a football match on that particular date.

The last murder was of the Leeds University student Jacqueline Hill in Headingley a district very popular with students. I had a tiny flat in Headingly where I kept my medical records, and this was quite close to the murder site. I was questioned again, and the police became quite excited when they learnt I had trained in Newcastle and had a flat close to the last crime. I was playing snooker with three friends in a snooker club in Leeds at the material time, but a group of six police officers came to interrogate my friends at their homes. It was not unusual to find the police had set up roadblocks and interviewed car drivers en mass at night.

From time to time, I was asked to do domiciliary visits in Chapeltown, then a red-light district of Leeds. This was always followed by a police visit as all cars entering and leaving that area had their registration numbers taken.

The Ripper murders were well spaced out in time with some longish gaps in between. I had been seeing a man privately over the previous three or four years. He worked in Saudi Arabia and after a 6 months intensive work schedule would take a sex holiday in either Thailand or Kenya. On returning to the Yorkshire Dales where he had a small cottage he would lie on his bed and over the bed was a bank of fluorescent lights. Having undressed, he would lie on the bed naked and wait for any adverse developments on his 'best bits'. After two or three weeks of this intense surveillance he would become increasingly suspicious that something was not right and phoned for a private appointment to check his 'privates'. I never found any evidence of disease and he always seemed reassured by this. It was, however, strange behaviour. It occurred to me that this man could be the Ripper and his relatively long exits from the UK could explain the gaps between the various Ripper murders. I anguished what to do. I had a duty of confidentiality to the patient but there was also a duty to society. I discussed my conflict with the Medical Protection Society – medico-legal advisors and my medical insurers. I was told I should discuss the matter with the police. I also sought advice from the British Medical Association. This advice concurred with that of the Medical Protection Society.

After phoning the police a young detective sergeant came to talk to me. He pressed me hard for the patient's name and address but obviously I could not divulge these data. The young police officer told me he was very frustrated by the police enquiry and felt that his hands were tied by the senior officer leading this investigation. He was particularly concerned that all the evidence and data that had been collected had just been stored in hundreds of boxes with no attempt to analyse and look for links and identify names of those coming up frequently. It subsequently emerged that the Ripper was interviewed several times by the police but because he did not have a Northeast accent, was not troubled further. I had the dates when my patient had seen me over the previous 2 or 3 years and happily for the patient there was no correlation between these dates and the dates of the murders when my patient on balance was abroad.

Things were getting hysterical in Leeds in the meantime. I was giving a seminar on dermatology to about 20 medical students when the police barged in and took one of my male students for questioning, his only crime being that he came from the Northeast and had a beard.

I used to see my private patients in an upstairs bedroom. I converted this bedroom into a surgery and after a session at home I would dictate the letters and my wife would sit in the bow window of the surgery at night typing the letters until quite late. There was no IT in those days. I would then sign the letters and she would walk along the street for 150 yards or so to the letter box at the end of the road. Sometimes, however, she was too tired and I would post the letters. Shortly after the Ripper's last murder in Headingley I walked to the post box just before midnight. As I was coming back a white car drove along the road and parked under a streetlight. I got a very good look at the man who was fairly smartly dressed with dark hair and a dark beard. The man locked the car and began walking further down the street away from my house – rather odd behaviour I thought for this time of night. Was he having an affair with a woman in an adjacent street I wondered? I took the car's registration number and the following day my neighbour said she had been burgled and the burglars had emptied her freezer. I gave her the registration number of the car to give to the police who subsequently told my neighbour the plates on the car were false but there was no police follow up. Shortly afterwards the Ripper was arrested in Sheffield largely because he was driving a car in a red-light area with false number plates.

I could not wait to see the photograph of the suspect. When I did there was no doubt, I had seen the Ripper, Peter Sutcliffe in the flesh that night. Had he seen my wife in the surgery window? Had he seen her posting letters on her own at night and could she have been his next intended victim? My wife and I will never know.

Two or three years later I met Dr Jeremy Coid one of the forensic psychiatrists in the case. Jeremy was strongly of the opinion that Sutcliffe had schizophrenia but despite the medical evidence that Sutcliffe had a psychosis he was not allowed to plead on grounds of diminished responsibility. He was found guilty of murder and was sent initially to an ordinary high security prison. He was later transferred to Broadmoor, a prison for the criminally insane, but spent the latter part of his life in an ordinary prison which he found more uncomfortable and his transfer from Broadmoor was against his wishes. Controversially he was awarded approximately £100,000 following an assault in prison leading to a severe eye injury to one eye. I gather he died in Durham jail of covid having elected not to receive any treatment.

BRAZIL

I was invited to give a talk at a World Congress of Dermatology held in Rio De Janeiro. My wife and I were warned about the high crime rate in Brazil and in Rio in particular where it has been estimated there are about a million people actively engaged in crime. The favelas (slums) were home to these criminals and were situated just behind the plush hotels on the sea front. The sewage from the favelas went directly into the sea and the discoloration this caused was evident from the hotel bedroom window. Even so some of the delegates chose to swim in this very polluted ocean.

On the first day a German dermatologist went for a swim in the early morning. He had been careful to remove his watch but had forgotten about his wedding ring. He was mugged by three men and fortunately said his ring came off easily. He was sure he would have lost a finger if this was not the case. On the same day another delegate went down to the spa in his bathrobe and swimming trunks carefully locking all his valuables including his passport, money, credit card, watch and aeroplane tickets in his safe, putting the key to his safe in his bathrobe pocket. He locked the robe in the spa and enjoyed a relaxing morning. A horrendous situation greeted him when he went to put his bathrobe back on. He found his locker had been broken into and the key to his room and safe had also gone. When he eventually got into his room, he found all his valuables had been stolen as well as his clothes. All he had in the world were his swimming trunks and flip flops.

On the way from the airport to the hotel, we had some concerns. We had been warned that one taxi scam was for the driver to say that he had a flat tyre and when the boot was opened for the spare all the luggage would be stolen by accomplices. Horror of horrors as we were driving over a very high viaduct, the taxi driver announced he had a flat tyre! My wife and I were sharing a taxi with Rod Hay a dermatologist from London and later dean of medicine in Belfast. For a moment we all thought we were to be thrown off the viaduct, but no, the taxi driver had a genuine flat tyre, and the spare was bald. We ended up buying the driver a new tyre.

On the penultimate night my wife and I were invited to a party at the conference president's apartment over-looking Copacabana Beach which is illuminated every night. I am told that this is not only so people can continue their sporting activities, but also serves as a security measure.

Security men with dogs greeted us at the apartment entrance and we entered a lift which took us directly up three or four floors and into the president's quarters which were both luxurious and a bit strange at the same time. Waiters wearing white gloves proffered drinks and we were introduced to the president's wife who was ugly to the point of fascination. There were many paintings on the wall, and some were standing against the wall. All looked like they had been executed by a child of no more than 10 years old whereas in reality they were the work of the president's wife.

Larry Parish a distinguished American dermatologist and editor of a well-known dermatological journal arrived. He was targeted by the wife who took him around the art exhibition. It became clear to us, but not to Larry at this stage that everything in the apartment was for sale. The wife escorted Larry around her 'masterpieces' and he was polite. In the end she asked which painting did he like the best. With some difficulty he selected one and the wife said, "You will have it". "No no" protested Larry all to no avail, she flicked her fingers and a waiter wearing white gloves was instructed to wrap it up. "That's a thousand dollars" she said to an astonished and now speechless Larry who protested he had no money with him. "I will take a credit card" was the reply and Larry explained he did not have his credit card with him either. "You can send me a cheque when you get back to the States" and Larry promised he would, and he did. Larry told me he displays this painting in his consulting rooms to remind him of his stupidity.

By now the room was full and alcohol was flowing freely. Soon the Finnish delegates, who always seem to get drunk at conference receptions, before anyone else began singing their national songs. Dinner was eventually served about midnight. As midnight was approaching the president's wife sat down at the piano and rendered a selection of songs from Cats – badly! Her musical standards were similar to her artistic ability. My wife and I had had enough. The problem was that the piano and pianist were situated adjacent to the lift the only obvious exit. We had to wait for the music to stop and it seemed a very uncomfortable and embarrassing age before the music finished but the pianist had no shame.

After the conference we had a short add on holiday. My wife wanted to stay at a particular hotel she had read about in Manaus. Inflation was rampant in Brazil at the time and most commerce was done in US dollars. I paid 150 US dollars to stay two nights in this particular special hotel situated on the banks of the Amazon.

As we drove by taxi from the airport to the hotel, we saw an army of workers painting the kerbs white and flags were flapping from a mile of flagpoles. We checked in our hotel and wandered down to the lobby intending to have a walk around the gardens. An amazing scene met our eyes. The lobby was full of military men bedecked in gold braid and medals and there was a gun boat moored opposite the hotel. This was a meeting of seven South American Presidents, and it turned out that my wife and I were the only non-political guests in the hotel. Someone had been bounced out of their room for 150 US dollars. The hotel lights suddenly went out and chaos followed because of the concern that this could be a prelude to a terrorist attack. Security men were racing up and down corridors shouting to each other as they went. It became evident, however, that it was just a routine power cut, common at that time in Brazil, but embarrassing for the Brazilian presidential host.

Our room opened onto a large, magnificent swimming pool and I went for a swim the following morning. I was the only guest in the pool and watched the opening session of the Presidents' meeting which took place at the pool side from my aquatic viewpoint. It was all very grand. National anthems were played and there was much hand shaking.

Later that day we met a friend, a dermatologist from Pontefract, Donald Williamson and his wife Sheila in Manaus. We went around the market with a guide. Donald was always fascinated by electrical gadgets and found something he wanted to buy. He asked his wife for some money. All their money was in a wallet in his wife's handbag. She went to fetch out the wallet and found that it had gone via a very neat incision in the leather; she never felt a thing. We went to the police who asked how much money had been stolen - "About 200 US dollars," Donald said. "No," said the police, "it was 2,000 US." An argument ensued. The police wanted to issue a document stating 2,000 dollars had been stolen and Donald was to pay them 500 dollars in the meantime. He refused and eventually the police let him go. The following day as he was boarding the flight back to Rio two police officers in plain clothes, both bedecked with gold watches and gold necklaces pulled Donald aside and once more tried to coerce him. Again, he refused. He just caught the flight in time.

Postscript:

Brazil was and still is riddled with corruption, which is everywhere involving politicians the police, gangs in favelas and even children. There are a few very rich people in Brazil and millions of very poor people. The rich however, are almost in prison. They are afraid to ride about the cities in their cars lest they get kidnapped and have to be protected like the president of the conference by security men who may be corrupt themselves.

This is a state of affairs that cannot persist and, in my opinion will not persist. Sadly there is no sign of the situation ending any time soon.

ABOUT THE AUTHOR

I grew up in Sheffield and after a Grammar School education trained in Newcastle at the Durham University Medical School when I was then just 17 years of age – far too young in retrospect. To my amazement and to the amazement of my parents, I won undergraduate prizes in anatomy, ophthalmology and dermatology and a distinction in public health. I also gained a bursary to read for a degree in physiology and subsequently gained a first-class honours degree in this subject.

My decision to become a dermatologist was influenced both by Professor J T Ingram, the first professor of dermatology in England and also by his deputy Dr Gunter Holti. Dr Holti was Swiss and despite his nationality served in the British Army during the second World War because he was horrified by what was happening in Europe. After the war Gunter took his medical degree in Leeds.

In those days a career in dermatology demanded a higher level knowledge of general medicine and after a few locum jobs I worked as a senior house officer and registrar in medicine in Ipswich for Dr John Paulley arguably the father of modern gastroenterology and the leading light in the creation of Buckingham University – the first private university in the UK.

Dr Paulley was very interested in psychosomatic aspects of medicine and his teaching influenced me to develop a special interest in the emotional, psychological and psychiatric aspects of dermatology. Later posts were as medical registrar at Doncaster Royal Infirmary where the volume of work was overwhelming, but the medical experience exceptional. I took the MRCP (Member of The Royal College of Physicians in London) examination 8 times before successfully gaining this qualification necessary to become a consultant dermatologist. I was later appointed tutor and then consultant dermatologist at the General Infirmary in Leeds (LGI). My predecessor at the Infirmary was Dr S T Anning who told me he had taken the membership thirteen times! It was indeed a very difficult examination in those far off days and was alleged to have a pass rate of less than 5% at that time. In addition to sessions at the Infirmary I undertook two sessions per week at Harrogate District Hospital and I also had inpatients at St James's Hospital in Leeds (Jimmys). I undertook private work and ended up with more private patients than I could happily manage.

Besides an interest in psychodermatology, I was one of the first dermatologists to use lasers in dermatology mainly to treat children with port wine stains. I went on to develop, what I think is one of the best laser units in the NHS and trained a whole generation of juniors in this art. I was a founder member of the British Medical Laser Association and co-founder of the European Society of Psychodermatology with Professor Peter Berner then professor of psychiatry in Vienna and was elected president of this society for 4 years.

I was also elected president of the Dowling Club, an international club with nearly 700 members and took a group of senior dermatologists but mostly junior dermatologists to visit dermatological centres in Mexico, San Francisco, Amsterdam, Utrecht and Marburg.

I was in demand as a lecturer all over the world and gave lectures mainly on psychodermatology and laser treatment in more than 30 different countries. I have published over 100 clinical and scientific papers in peer reviewed journals and have contributed to chapters in several dermatological textbooks. I retired from clinical dermatology in 2000 but continued an interest in medico-legal work.

In the springtime of my senescence in 2010, I decided to change course completely and bought some land in Southern Tuscany on which I established a truffle farm. Eleven years later I am still waiting to produce my first significant harvest of black winter truffles. Hope springs eternal.

Professor Sir George Pickering, one time professor of medicine in Cambridge, asserted in one of his books that there were only two opportunities to write during a busy life – first was if you were in prison and secondly if you were ill – so now in addition to being an Italian peasant I chancing my arm as a writer whilst my metastatic prostate cancer remains in remission. I hope you have enjoyed what I have written and look forward to your feedback which may or may not encourage me to write a bit more.

Ingram Content Group UK Ltd.
Milton Keynes UK
UKHW020626100523
421505UK00013B/225

9 781739 123321